# Fasting in Islam

## by

## Shaykh Fadhlalla Haeri

Zahra Publications

Rasooli Centre
PO Box 5064
Wierda Park
Centurion 0149
Gauteng
Republic of South Africa

Zahra Trust
P.O Box 1021
London W2 4JQ
England

Zahra Publications
P.O Box 12300
Karachi 75500
Pakistan

Typesetting by Pixel Graphics
Printed and bound in Pakistan by
Asian Packages (Pvt.) Ltd.
Karachi-Pakistan

Special thanks to Liaquat Ali of Progas Pakistan

ISBN  1-919897-22-4 (Fasting in Islam)

Email : zahrapublications@yahoo.com
www.nuradeen.com

# Contents

# Acknowledgements

This book would not have come about without the considerable time and energy spent by several people, in particular, Hajj Ahmed Mikel!, Zainab Hussain Haeri, Muna Bilgrami, Hasan Joban and Dr. Ya'qub Zaki, whose editorial input was most helpful. My thanks are due to all of them.

# Introduction

This book was written for the present-day Muslim, with the objective of making the practice of fasting, or *sawm*, understandable and easy to follow.

In the past, Muslim communities and societies simply carried on the rituals and practices they had inherited, while the younger generations absorbed and followed the same patterns. With the present dispersion of Muslims to countries all over the world and the subsequent multi-cultural and multi-lingual environments in which they find themselves, I felt that a book encompassing the main practices and meanings of fasting would be timely.

The main aim of this book is to cover all aspects of the Islamic faith that relate and connect to fasting, taking into account the outer advantage for the practitioner, as well as the subtler inner benefits.

The principal goal has been to communicate the practices of fasting for easy and understandable use so that in time the reader will realise the numerous benefits that can be gained from fasting and the transformative effects of this spiritual and physical practice.

In the first chapter we take a brief look at the history of fasting, followed by a discussion of the health benefits of fasting in chapter two. Chapter three examines the verses in the Qur'an that instruct us to fast and relate topics, such as the various types of fasting. After the Qur'an we naturally turn to the Sunnah, or life-pattern of the Prophet, which is primarily recorded in the body of *hadith*. Chapter four, therefore, offers a comprehensive selection of *hadith* on all aspects of *sawm*.

In chapter five we enumerate all the rules regulating the fast according to Ja'fari law (the school of the Ahl al-Bayt). In chapter six we look at the same rules according to the four Sunni schools of law. It will be noticed that any difference between the Ja'fari or

Ahl al-Bayt school and the Sunni schools are minor, and should, therefore, not be a cause of sectarian battle. We still find some people, however, who continue to engage in futile, hair-splitting theological debates, rather than witness the greatness of Islam and spread tolerance amongst Muslims.

Ramadan is singled out as a special time during which supplication to Allah is most effective and so in chapter seven we reproduce some recommended *du'as*. Ramadan is, of course, the blessed month during which the Qur'an was first revealed. Thus, in the eighth chapter we dwell on the meaning of the 'Night of Determination' (*Laylat al-Qadr*), as revealed in the Qur'anic chapter, Surat al-Qadr. Finally, in chapter nine, both the broader and inner aspects of fasting are explored. Fasting in Islam is not simply a matter of withholding from food and drink. Its ultimate purpose is inner purification, awareness, and sincere worship of Allah, the All-Encompassing Creator of all known and unknown worlds.

I pray that the reader will absorb and apply what is relevant and realise the transformative dimension of our great *Din*.

# Chapter One

## Fasting Through the Ages

The desire to fast seems to be deeply rooted in human consciousness. Fasting has been resorted to for cultural or political reasons as much as for maintaining physical and mental health. More specifically, fasting has been a devotional practice in most religious and spiritual movements throughout the ages.

Islam has perfected the practice of abstinence and fasting as a means of self-purification and worship. The act of restraining the self purifies and enhances awareness and sensitivity at physical, mental and spiritual levels. The seeker realizes the weakness of the self and is gratified by the discipline, restriction and prohibitions, for these limitations are windows to Allah's limitlessness.

### AN OVERVIEW

The word 'fast' in English comes from the Teutonic 'fastan', which means 'firm' in the sense of 'to hold fast, be firm, to observe [something] strictly or guard.' The verb 'fastan' means keeping or observing a rule of some kind and maintaining strict obedience to a law. The specific application of this meaning is associated with abstinence from food, and after a time, the abstention from food as a religious observance or as a ceremonial expression of grief became the accepted meaning.

In some cultures, such as the Indians of North America, fasting is held in high esteem, while many tribes of Brazil and the peoples of the Pacific Islands have used it as a rite of initiation. It was once common for hunters to fast before setting out in pursuit of game. Fasting to mark puberty is still a widespread practice among some American Indian Tribes, and is observed as a preliminary rite to marriage among some communities prior to marriage. Several cultures prescribe fasting as a rite of mourning, such as those in the Andaman Islands, Fiji, Samoa, China, Korea and Africa. In general, we find whenever human beings require or seek heightened awareness or greater closeness to their core or essence, fasting is used as a key practice to achieve this end.

Ancient Egyptians, Greek, Roman, and Chinese cultures practised fasting to cure various illnesses. The Egyptians believed that fasting three days a month helped to preserve good mental and physical health. The Greeks learned the virtues of fasting from the Egyptians and fasted before battle and the Romans followed suit. Socrates and Plato are known to have regularly performed fasts of ten days duration. Today in the West, fasting is used by alternative and naturopathic systems of medicine and healing for curing a host of acute and chronic diseases and as a useful catalyst in helping the body mobilize its own natural immune system.

During the twentieth century fasting has sometimes been used as a tool of political and social protest by individuals as well as groups. During the national struggles for independence from colonial rule, several leaders of the third world in Asia and Africa resorted to fasting to highlight their plight and struggle, often with some success.

In the religions of the East fasting has been practiced for spiritual purification and cleansing from sin. Manu stressed that the practice of fasting was utilized in order to acquire control over the senses. Hindu masters recommended a restraint on speech and actions and a total ban on injury to any created being. Gautama Buddha prescribed a middle path for attaining spiritual goals, avoiding the extremes of asceticism or luxury. Most monks, however, would follow austere regimes and fast for several days at a time, patiently bearing mental and physical weakness as a devotional practice.

The Old Testament abounds in references to fasting. David wept and chastened his soul with fasting. The Prophet Moses fasted from all food and drink for forty days and nights when he ascended the mount to receive the tablets of the covenant of his

Lord. Ezra, the prophet of the Children of Israel, fasted in order to obtain guidance from his Lord. Daniel fasted for three weeks, seeking his Lord by prayer and supplication.

The Jews observe six obligatory fasts during the year, one of which (Yom Kippur – the Day of Atonement) is prescribed in the Old Testament as a two-day fast. Yom Kippur derives from similar linguistic roots as *Yawm al-Kaffarah*, both of which mean the same thing, i.e. repentance, as Arabic and Hebrew have a common Semitic root. Moses descended with the Torah on Yom Kippur just as the Qur'an was revealed on *Laylat al-Qadr*, the Night of Determination or Power, during the month of Ramadan.

The New Testament contains numerous references to fasting and vigils. St. Jerome wrote: 'The fiery darts of Satan are to be quenched and deadened by the rigour of vigils and fasting.' Jesus is reported in Matthew to recommend sincere and cheerful fasting which became a normal practice for his disciples.

The institution of fasting and abstinence from certain foods in Christianity has its origin in the New Testament as it relates to the fasting of Jesus' disciples for several days during Lent, the forty-day period before Easter. The duration of the fast during Lent varied throughout the ages until forty days accompanied by strict rules became the norm. At first only one meal a day was allowed, and not before three in the afternoon, but gradually the time was brought forward to mid-day. Meat, fish, eggs, milk, cheese and butter were absolutely forbidden, but later on small amounts of these foods were allowed in the morning and evening.

Additional fasts were introduced later in different parts of the Church, such as the fast of Rogation Days, the Ember Weeks, the Whitsun Week, and fasts were also ordained by the Roman Catholic Church. Considerable variations in the practice of fasting is noticed between the Orthodox Church, the Eastern Orthodox Church and the Reformed Churches of Europe.

Over time there has been a gradual mitigation in the frequency and rigour of the fasts and abstinences prescribed by Church laws due to extenuating circumstances such as age, health, poverty, hard or continued labour and changing social conditions. Today few are obliged to fast strictly, while some are excused even from abstinence. Roman Catholic legislation further provides for dispensations to be granted by the Church authorities. The overall result is that the practice of fasting has declined and is almost forgotten as a religious exercise.

## THE ISLAMIC FAST

For Muslims fasting, or *'sawm'* in Arabic, was commanded in the Qur'an as a major obligatory spiritual discipline for the duration of the month of Ramadan. The Arabic word for fasting is derived from the root, *'sama'*, meaning to abstain from food, drink, smoking, sensual gratifications, wrong actions, harmful intentions, thoughts, words and deeds.

Islamic fasting is obligatory for one month in every lunar year, that is, Ramadan, the ninth month in the Islamic calendar. All healthy adults are expected to adhere to the proper rules of fasting. In addition to this obligatory fast, there are many optional fasts, some of which occur regularly every week or month, and some that are scattered throughout the year. These fasts are *Sunnah*, or the practice of the Prophet. Fasting is also used as a penance for breaking an oath and as a compensation for some other religious obligation.

The fast of Ramadan begins with the physical sighting of the new moon. Throughout the month a Muslim may not eat or drink from daybreak (when a fine strip of light may be seen on the horizon) until the sun has set. Before dawn a small meal (*suhur*) is usually recommended to be taken, although not obligatory, and just before the sunset (*maghrib*) prayer the fast is traditionally broken with dates and water, to be immediately followed by the prayer. Later on a larger meal is partaken by the entire family, often shared with relatives, friends and guests.

The daily fast is begun by formulating the intention to perform the fast as a rite by making a clear intention (*niyyah*) to observe the fast. No one should fast if their health cannot sustain it or if a fast should threaten one's health. Pregnant and nursing women whose health may be harmed are exempted, as are those who are travelling away from home. When health is restored or other conditions for breaking the fast are removed (such as menstruation) then the person is expected to make up the fast later during the course of the year. The rules and conditions for Islamic fasting are given in chapters five and six.

Ramadan offers the believer an opportunity to mark an end to indulgence, or at least to impose a clear limit to it, day after day for the duration of a month. This daily restraint breaks the habitual patterns of the self and constitutes a purification both of body and spirit, which brings about renewal of strength and greater spiritual awareness. Each and every ritualistic practice of Islam disciplines the individual and strengthens Muslim society if applied thoroughly.

Every year the month of Ramadan falls at different times because the lunar calendar is shorter than the solar by approximately ten days. This means that as the period of the fast is brought forward annually, Ramadan will fall during all seasons of the year in a gradual progression. Despite the strict rules and restraint induced by the fast, Ramadan is usually a joyful time for Muslims everywhere. The last ten nights of the month, particularly the odd nights, are the spiritual highlights of Ramadan, for one of these nights is *Laylat al-Qadr*, the Night of Determination, in which the Qur'an was first revealed to the Prophet.

Ramadan comes to a close with the celebrations and prayers of Eid al-Fitr. On this day a Muslim will give appropriate alms to the poor, and families gather for a light morning repast after the congregational prayer. The Eid prayer, performed outdoors, is followed by a discourse delivered by the prayer leader after which people exchange good wishes and celebrate their success in performing a most important act of worship and attaining a heightened awareness and purposefulness in life.

# Chapter Two

## Health, Diet and Fasting

The environment, our life-style and nutrition play a crucial role in determining our overall health. The affluence that capitalism and technology have brought to parts of the world during the twentieth century has improved living conditions and life expectancy, but also undermined certain qualities of life. Denatured foodstuffs (like white bread and white sugar), sedentary lifestyles, a hectic pace of life, environmental pollution together with many other factors have brought about high levels of pressure and stress on contemporary humankind. For people living in large cities, these negative influences are most concentrated. No one is immune to their effects.

## FOOD AND SPIRITUALITY

A better quality of life, self-development, higher consciousness or spiritual development cannot be pursued with a diseased and ailing body. Disease and illness, however, are signals and warnings of physical or mental imbalance and thus need attention and remedial treatment. The Qur'an indicates the importance of what we eat and how we eat it:

> And in the earth are tracts and gardens of vines and fields sown with corn, and palm-trees growing out of single roots and otherwise, watered with the same water, and yet some We make more excellent than others in fruits; Verily in this there are signs for people who understand. (13:4)

> Eat of the good things We have provided you with and exceed not in it. (20:81)

> And eat and drink For He loves not those who go to excess. (7:31)

The middle path, moderation and constant awareness are the marks of a sincere seeker. Our present culture, however, is obsessed with increase. Thus excess weight and obesity are prevalent in wealthy societies. The Prophet said that there is nothing worse than a stomach stuffed with permissible (i.e. lawful) food. Imam 'Ali said: 'Never eat unless you are hungry; always leave a meal while still desiring to eat.' In addition the Prophet has said to leave one third of the stomach empty and the other two thirds for water and food.

For a serious seeker eating is an act of worship, for it oils and maintains the vehicle of one's journey. Knowledge and care is called for in deciding what to eat, when to eat and how to eat. It is said that food is for the spirit while prayer is for the body, because the outer nourishes and sustains the inner and the inner nourishes and sustains the outer. Without the body the spirit would not manifest.

## VARIETIES OF FOOD

Allah says in the Qur'an:

> Let man consider his food. We send down water pouring, then We split the earth and cause to grow therein grain, grapes, herbs, olives, dates, gardens thick with trees, fruits and grasses, provision for you and your livestock. (80:24-32)

> He is the One Who created trellised and untrellised gardens, dates, various edible grains and other standing crops, olives and pomegranates, similar and dissimilar. Eat of its fruit when it bears fruit. (6:141)

These verses demonstrate the wondrous nature of food and how we are provided for with edible substances from creation. We need to learn when they should be eaten and in what combinations and quantities, as well as methods of preparation.

## TRADITIONAL PATTERNS OF EATING

People who lived in evolved traditional cultures have over the centuries developed generally sound dietary practices suited to their particular environments and ways of life. In our time many dietary habits that were specific to a society or tribe have slipped into other cultures because of easy communication, travel, transport, trade and the concomitant desire to emulate 'healthy' or – 'wealthy'– peoples. It is not easy, therefore, to discern distorted, harmful or out of context eating practices. People who have maintained traditional patterns of eating born of long experience and wisdom are now the exception rather than the rule. Nowadays most foods are available to wealthy nations all year round, regardless of season, courtesy of modern transport and technology.

## THE ETIQUETTE (*adab*) OF EATING AND DRINKING

How we eat food is a good indication of our awareness and sensitivity regarding this most important action. Young children mess about and behave in an understandably animalistic manner when they eat. As we grow older and wiser we realise the importance of choosing our food carefully, its quantity and quality, our mental attitude while eating and the speed with which we consume our food. If one eats intelligently, varying the varieties of food while restraining excessive appetites then sufficient pleasure and nourishment may be obtained. Stress, anger, distractions and other emotional disturbances whilst eating are a sure way to reduce the benefits of our food.

The Prophetic teaching provides us with a whole system of courtesy and etiquette regarding food and eating. The purpose of taking in food is to maintain life, whose ultimate purpose is the awareness and knowledge of the Life-giver, Allah, the Exalted. From this knowledge emerges an attitude of contentment and celebration of life's experiences.

1. *The following list of basic recommendations are derived from the practice of the Prophet. One should:*

a) Wash the hands before a meal. When there are guests, the host begins by washing his own hands.

b) Wash the hands and mouth after a meal.

c) If there are guests, the host should begin eating before the guests and finish after them (so as not to rush them).

d) Begin the meal by saying *Bismillahi'r-Rahmani'r-Rahim* (In the Name of Allah, the Beneficent, the Merciful), thereby dedicating the act to a higher purpose.

e) Eat the meal in a spirit of gratitude and enjoyment. One should be on one's best behaviour at the table, exhibiting tolerance and consideration for the others.

f) Eat with the right hand only.

g) If one is eating with the fingers it is best to eat with three fingers (the index finger, the middle finger and the thumb).

h) Eat the food which is in front of one, i.e. within easy reach.

i) Take small bites and chew well and slowly.

j) Not eat hurriedly or hasten to leave the table.

k) Use a toothpick after a meal and if possible use a toothbrush or *miswak*.

l) Sit straight whilst eating, not reclining or resting one's back on cushions.

m) Rest after a meal and if possible recline, preferably with the right leg over the left.

n) Avoid eating when full or not hungry. One should eat with a healthy appetite and stop before feeling full.

o) Eat heavy meals at noontime only, unless there is a valid reason for otherwise. The evening meal should generally be the lighter of the two.

p) Eat in company, especially with family, servants and friends.

q) Eat the evening meal early.

r) Say little whilst eating or drinking, and avoid interrupting meals to attend to other activities.

## 2. *The following are recommended when drinking:*

a) Sip water slowly rather than gulp it down.

b) Remember Allah before drinking and praise Him when finished.

c) Drink water three swallows at a time successively.

d) Drink water with relish and enjoyment.

e) Remember Imam Husayn's thirst in the last days of his martyrdom at Karbala.

## 3. *The following are considered reprehensible when eating:*

a) Eating while performing other actions or being distracted.

b) Eating too much or to one's full capacity. Leaving one third of the stomach empty is best.

c) Looking in the face of another while they are eating.

d) Eating food that is too hot and blowing on it to cool it.

e) Eating a great variety of fruit, vegetables or other food stuffs at the same time.

f) Eating excess meat or not eating meat at all for forty days.

g) Eating before taking a ritual bath (*ghusl*) after sexual intercourse. If one be unable to perform the ritual bath, one should at ieast cleanse the nose and rinse the mouth.

h) Eating while walking.

## 4. *The following are considered reprehensible when drinking:*

a) Drinking too much water.

b) Drinking water after eating, especially after eating the noon meal or after a meal that is rich in fat.

c) Drinking from a place, a cup or container which is broken or from the side of the handle.

d) Drinking with the left hand.

## FASTING AS A CURE

Fasting is probably one of the oldest known methods of healing the body. Many people and have used fasting as a means to detoxify the body and to cure disease. Fasting does indeed cleanse the body and allow us to assimilate subtler forms of nourishment by releasing the energy that would have been used for digestion and using this in tandem with the natural process of healing.

After the first few days of fasting, providing that one is not stuffing oneself in between with inappropriate foods, the appetite fades and we find that our anxiety and attachment to food begins to lessen. All the eliminative systems of the body, such as the skin, the lungs, the liver, kidneys and bowels become more active. This is often reflected in bad breath, body odour, and foul smelling body wastes. These unpleasant side-effects signify that the digestive system is detoxifying itself and that the biochemical and mineral balance in the body tissues is changing. This process is greatly enhanced if one eats plenty of fresh fruit and drinks water and vegetable juices. After a few days of fasting the process of autolysis begins, whereby dead and unhealthy cells are broken down and remetabolized.

For over a thousand years Muslim physicians have used fasting to cure a number of different diseases, including smallpox. Avicenna (Ibn Sina) mentioned fasting as a therapeutic technique in his Canon. Four hundred years before the birth of Jesus, Hippocrates prescribed fasting to heal illness. During the Renaissance, Venetian over-indulgence in food and drink and gluttony became so excessive that the rise in sickness and even death of wealthy citizens became a public disgrace. During the eighteenth century several European physicians advocated fasting in treating epilepsy, ulcers, plethora, cataracts, scurvy and malignant ulcers. Fasting as prevention of illness and complete abstention from eating during illness became established as a healing method for numerous common diseases.

In the United States during the 19th century the question of toxins and degenerative diseases became an important issue for which fasting was considered a major cure. The idea of toxicity as the cause of disease found more favour with naturopathic physicians than with the allopaths, who were firmly convinced of the germ origin of disease. Fasting was prescribed for stomach and intestinal disorders, obesity, dropsy, various infections and inflammations, the elimination of physical weakness and flabbiness as well as for the improvement of morale.

Proponents and practitioners of fasting today employ different forms of fasting. They may allow only water for specified periods of time, from three to 30 days, or the fast may be supplemented by a monofood diet, such as certain types of fruits or fruit and vegetable juices. According to these methods the therapy, if successful, will provoke a 'healing' or 'detoxification crisis', which is the temporary exacerbation of the symptoms followed by a rapid and complete recovery. Adherents believe that one can expel suppressed or latent toxins remaining from old diseases if cleansing is continued. These latent toxins are often believed to be due to the side-effects of drug therapies.

Fasting is considered to offer a physiological rest for the digestive tract and central nervous system while normalizing the metabolism. During a fast the kidney preserves potassium and sugar in the blood which is an important element in ensuring that the person fasting maintains a state of well-being. When there is no food to digest, the human body needs only a minimum of energy to carry out other functions, such as repleneshing old cells and eliminating toxic residues.

Chinese medical practitioners of their ancient and effective system have a lucid and balanced approach to detoxification of the body through the use of fasting. Chinese medicine has developed two broad categories of therapy over the centuries. One is tonification or building up deficiencies and the other is reduction or elimination of excess. Fasting is a process of eliminating excess. In people with a strong constitution fasting may be an appropriate therapy. In people with a weak or deficient constitution, using an eliminative process such as fasting could cause complications. In such cases sound judgement must be used to decide whether to eliminate the excess first, tonifying the deficiency, or do both simultaneously.

The Chinese system of medicine is holistic, based on the idea that no single part can be understood except in its relation to the whole. A symptom is observed as a part of a person's entire, physical state of being rather than as traced to a cause. In illness the symptom is only one part of an imbalance that can be observed in other aspects of a person's physical state. A person who is well or 'in harmony' has no distressing symptoms and expresses mental, physical and spiritual balance.

The dietary habits of many ordinary rural Muslim folk throughout the world, whether in China, Hunza or the Atlas Mountains of North Africa, are in concordance with the best guidelines for a healthy diet advocated by most modern-day nutritionists and naturopaths. They eat and drink in moderation, in season, and only a limited variety of foods. All fruits and vegetables are either fresh or dry, while processed or canned food is simply unavailable. Their lifestyles are far from sedentary and physical activity is almost continuous.

Modern urban-dwelling Muslims, however, are subject to the same negative factors that afflict all cities throughout the world. The stress of pollution, refined food products, excessive amounts of fried 'fast' foods, as well as the heavy use of spices and food additives, combined with the frenetic pace of life, social alienation and urban anonymity, take their toll on health and well-being.

Our urban modern way of life requires us to give special consideration to many factors that affect our health. Among the more important are:

- The quality of our food, water and air;

- Food combining and mixing, such as avoiding meals which mix concentrated carbohydrates with concentrated proteins;

- Avoiding processed foods such as bleached and refined flour products and sugar;

- Avoiding foods with preservatives, colourants and other artificial additives;

- Avoiding snacking between meals;

- Exercising regularly;

- Avoiding remaining deskbound and sitting in fixed positions at work or during travel.

Numerous unhealthy contemporary habits which are considered 'normal' and even desirable are unhealthy, and these include:

- Styles and materials of dress. Tight trousers, for example, are known to affect fertility in males; or clothing which is not protective enough or too synthetic material to allow the skin to respire sufficiently;

- Chemicals such as nail-varnish, deodorants, hairsprays and industrial soaps etc.;

- Colas and other artificially flavoured drinks;

- Foods containing preservatives, colourants, taste enhancers, artificial sweeteners;

- Drinking before or during a meal (the best is to drink half an hour before food or one hour after);

- Drinking anything that is ice-cold or too hot;

- Drugs, especially pain-relievers, cortico-steroids and sedatives;

- Cigarettes and alcohol.

The necessity for exercise, fresh air and sunshine cannot be over-emphasised. Deep regular breathing, brisk walks or other physically revitalizing activities are essential elements in creating and maintaining good health. Changing one's style of life to reduce stress can only improve one's capacity for better health and inner development.

During a fast the body heals and purifies itself. It is for this reason that to obtain the full benefit of Ramadan one must eat in moderation and care when fast-breaking. The choice of foods is as important as the quantity. It makes no sense to squander the opportunity for renewal and regeneration that Ramadan represents by indulging in indiscriminate eating as soon as the sun goes down. Applying this awareness frequently requires one to look beyond culturally ingrained eating patterns, in particular those that have developed in the last few decades as a result of affluence and the increased availability of highly processed and refined foods. From a healthy and vibrant physical state we can transcend our limitations to reach the higher elements within ourselves. We need a healthy body and mind to discover the light of the Eternal within us, which is the purpose of creation and the plan and design of the Loving Creator.

# Chapter Three

# The Qur'an on Fasting

The Qur'an is the foundation of revealed Divine ways and knowledge. For the wayfarer in this world it offers the comprehensive guide and code for proper conduct. The Qur'an is the ultimate, complete book of wisdom which fulfils the message of every prophet. Moving across the boundaries of time and space, this Divine revelation covers the heavens and earth, this life and the next, and time and timelessness, so that we may taste the vastness and unique Oneness behind all creational dualities. It is the voice of the Absolute so that one can deal wisely with all relative worldly experiences.

The Qur'anic verses cannot be easily classified by isolated topics, because of the inter-relationship and connection between intentions, actions, the seen and unseen and other dimensions of life. The individual being is closely connected with his society and the environment and his actions will have a far-reaching impact upon others, although this is not always easily perceivable.

The word for fasting (*sawm*) and its derivatives are mentioned some thirteen times in the Qur'an. Four of these twelve verses contain the command to fast in the month of Ramadan, five others deal with fasting either as an expiation for some wrong deed or as a compensation for the omission of an obligatory act; another verse praises the act of fasting, while yet another refers to the fast of Mary, the mother of Jesus, during her vow of silence. The abstention from talking to people enjoined upon the Prophet Zachariah is mentioned in the Qur'an without referring to it as fasting:

He said: My Lord! Give me a sign. He said: Your sign is that you will not speak to people for three nights though you are in sound health. (19:10)

The month of Ramadan is mentioned only once in the Qur'an along with the injunction to fast. The following verse praises the act of fasting:

Surely the men who submit and the women who submit, and the believing men and the believing women, and the obeying men and the obeying women, and the truthful men and the truthful women, and the humble men and the humble women, and the alms-giving men and the alms-giving women, and the fasting men and the fasting women, and the men who guard their private parts and the women who guard, and the men who remember Allah much and the women who remember – Allah has prepared for them forgiveness and a mighty reward. (33:35)

The next verse refers to the fast of Mary, mother of Jesus, who was ordered to refrain from speaking to people as a protection from idle questions about her situation regarding the birth of Jesus:

So eat and drink and refresh the eye. Then if you see any mortal, say: Surely I have vowed a fast to the Beneficent God, so I shall not speak to any man today. (19:26)

Of the four verses that specifically refer to fasting in Ramadan contained in the chapter of the Cow, the following three form the injunction and general guidelines, while the fourth gives us greater detail about conditions governing the fast:

O you who believe! Fasting is prescribed for you, as it was prescribed for those before you, so that you may guard (against evil). (2:183)

For a certain number of days; but whoever among you is sick or on a journey, then (he shall fast) a (like) number of other days; and those who are not able to do it may effect a redemption by feeding a poor man; so whoever does good spontaenously it is better for you; and that you fast is better for you if you know. (2:184)

The month of Ramadan is that in which the Qur'an was revealed, a guidance to men and clear proofs of the guidance and the distinction; therefore whoever of you is present in the month, he shall fast therein, and whoever is sick or upon a journey, then (he shall fast) a (like) number of other days; Allah desires ease for you, and He does not desire for you difficulty, and (He desires) that you should complete the number and that you should exalt the greatness of Allah for His having guided you and that you may give thanks. (2:185)

These three verses revealed together specify the obligation to fast the month of Ramadan. The first two verses are preparatory, reminding us that the practice of fasting has always been enjoined upon mankind. 'Those before you' refers to the followers of Moses, Jesus, and the earlier Prophets, culminating in the final Islamic revelation.

In verse 184 the word translated as 'redemption' (fidya) means replacing the fast with an acceptable substitute. Here it is a material one, food, which would satisfy a poor person. Thus may those for whom fasting is impossible or difficult due to age or serious illness fulfil their obligation. 'Allah desires ease for you and He does not desire hardship for you'. Substitution is obligatory, as is the dispensation given to the sick person or traveller, who must make up the fast at a later date.

As Islam is a life-transaction that can only flourish in community life, it is therefore preferable that one should fast within the calm conditions of one's home and familiar routine. If one has to travel during Ramadan, without intending to remain in one place for ten days or more, then according to both Ja'fari and Hanafi law they should not fast, whereas the other schools maintain it is optional. Although stability and short-term residence are conditions for normal fasting, persons whose livelihood depend on constant travel (which to them is therefore normal) are allowed to fast whilst on the move. Some Muslim scholars contend that verse 185 gives to a sick person or traveller only the dispensation or permission not to fast, but does not compel them to avoid fasting and that it is a matter of individual choice. According to Ja'fari law anyone in such a position is required not to fast during the prescribed days, but must fast an equivalent number of other days.

This is also the ruling of some of the great Companions, notably 'Abd ar-Raḥman ibn 'Awf, 'Umar ibn al-Khattab, 'Abdullah ibn 'Umar, Abu Hurayrah and 'Urwah ibn az-Zubayr. It has been related that 'Umar ibn al-Khattab ordered a man who had fasted while on a journey to repeat his fast. Yusuf ibn al-Habam related that he asked Ibn 'Umar about fasting while on a journey and Ibn 'Umar answered, 'If someone offered you a gift and you refused it, would not the one who offered it be angry? Not fasting when on a journey is Allah's gift to you.'

> It is made lawful for you to go in to your wives on the night of the fast. They are a raiment for you and you are a raiment for them; Allah knew that you acted unjustly to yourselves, so He turned to you in mercy and removed [the burden] from you. So now be in contact with them and seek what Allah has ordained for you, and eat and drink until the whiteness of the day becomes distinct from the blackness of the night a dawn, then complete the fast till nightfall, and touch them not while you keep to the mosques. These are the limits of Allah, so go not near them. Thus does Allah make clear His messages for men that they may keep their duty. (2:187)

Until the revelation of this verse Muslims used to abstain from sexual intercourse during the nights of the fast. It is related that the Messenger of Allah came to know of some youths who secretly indulged in sexual relations at night during Ramadan, whereupon Allah revealed this verse, making it permissible. However, all forms of sexual courting, foreplay and anything that may lead to ejaculation is prohibited during the actual fasting time of the days of Ramadan.

This ordinance recognizes human weakness and needs. Witness the fact that husbands and wives are described as being 'a raiment' for each other, that is, something that would clothe and protect each other. Thus the nature of the relationship of marriage is metaphorically described here as being one which gives a human being dignity, solace, and comfort. Sexual intercourse within marriage protects not only the emotional, physical and moral health of the individual, but also that of society. It is so basic a function of humankind that it even finds place within the purifying and elevating practice of fasting.

## THE MEANING OF RAMADAN

The month of Ramadan is the ninth month of the Islamic Lunar calendar and falls between Sha'ban and Shawwal. It is the only month mentioned in the Qur'an [2:185].

The ancient Arabs had named the lunar months according to certain social circumstances or natural events or conditions that prevailed at the time of their naming. Thus *Muharram* (meaning 'forbidden') was a month in which warfare was banned. The two months called *Jumada* (the first, *al-Awwal,* and the second, *al-Thani*), whose meaning conveys the sense of becoming hard or solid, were thus named because during these months wells or springs became low or 'hard'.

Although there is no clear concensus on the meaning of 'Ramadan', it is likely to be related to the verbal root form *'ramada'*, which means 'to bake' or 'to be heated up by the sun'. This verb was often used to describe the cooking process by which a whole sheep or goat would be baked in a pit in the ground, covered by hot ashes and scalding stones. Ramadan could have been the hottest point during the year, though because of the lunar nature of the Islamic calendar it actually falls at different times throughout the year as each year goes by (a difference of ten days). Some say that Ramadan means the month of 'heat', because one would be burning off one's wrong actions by total abstention and restriction.

## REVELATION OF THE QUR'AN

The Qur'an was 'sent down' (*'unzila'*) during the month of Ramadan. *Anzala,* meaning 'to cause to come down', is rooted in *nazala*, 'to descend from a height'. From *anzala* are derived the two terms *inzal* and *tanzil;* both mean 'revelation', but with subtle shadings in meaning. *Inzal* implies an instantaneous sending down, while *tanzil* implies sending down in a step-by-step fashion. In

Surat al-Baqarah (2:185) 'sent down' is directly connected to *inzal*: thus the phrase clearly implies that the light of the whole Qur'an descended during the month Ramadan, though it took a period of twenty-three years for it to become outwardly and physically manifest. Allah reveals in Surat al-Qadr (chapter 97):

> Surely We revealed it on the Night of Determination -
>
> And what will make you comprehend what the Night of Determination is?
>
> The Night of Determination is better than a thousand months.
>
> The Angels and the Spirit descend in it by the permission of their Lord – for every affair –
>
> Peace! it is till the break of dawn.

Allah also says:

> And certainly, We have brought them a Book which We have made clear with knowledge, a guidance and a mercy for a people who believe. Do they wait for aught but its final interpretation? On the day when its final interpretation comes about, those who neglected it aforetime will say: Indeed the messengers of our Lord brought the truth. (7:52-53)
>
> And this Qur'an is not such as could be forged by those besides Allah but it is a verification of that which preceded it and a setting forth in detail of the Book. There is no doubt in it, from the Lord of the worlds. Nay, they rejected that of which they had no comprehensive knowledge, and its final interpretation has not yet come to them. (10:37-39)
>
> And it is in the original Book with Us, truly elevated, full of wisdom. (43:4)
>
> It is on a preserved tablet.(85:22)

## FASTING AS A MEANS OF GLORIFYING AND THANKING ALLAH

> So that you may glorify Allah and His guidance that perhaps you may be grateful to Him.

There is a difference between glorifying Allah and thanking Him by fasting. It is when one embraces the real spirit of the fast, which is purifying oneself from material involvement and abstaining from the fulfilment of one's appetites, that a fast can be said to express gratitude. Glorification, however, does not depend on that essential spirit. Observing the form of the fast, whether with sincere intention or not, attests to the glory of Allah and His greatness because by embracing an act of self-denial one is still following His command.

## THE START OF FASTING

> Eat and drink until the white thread (of dawn) becomes distinct
> to you from the black thread (of night) at dawn.

There are two dawns: the first is known as the 'false dawn' (*subh al-kadhib*) because it vanishes within a short time. It is also called the 'tail of the wolf' because it looks like a raised vulpine tail. This false dawn is a beam of light, like a vertical column, which appears toward the end of night on the eastern horizon when the sun reaches a level of 18 degrees below the horizon. The second dawn, which is is known as the 'true dawn' (*subh al-sadiq*) comes when this vertical beam of light gives way to a horizontal line of light which looks as if a white thread has been stretched along the horizon. From that point on the horizon continues to brighten gradually until the sun rises above it.

## BREAKING THE FAST

> Then complete the fast till nightfall...

meaning maintain the fast until after the sun sets, when it will be permissible to break it. The cautious Muslims wait a few minutes longer until the redness of the sky has completely disappeared before they break the fast by drinking or eating something.

Some people may be tempted to continue fasting after sunset or even into the next day without food or drink. Although there is much inner joy in continuing one's heightened inner awareness by prolonged fasting, the Prophet's advice and recommendation is is to break the fast after every sunset as well as to eat and drink something before dawn. The Prophet always prescribed moderation and balance

## RETREAT

> And associate not with them while you are confined in the mosque.

Retreat to a mosque is a voluntary act of worship performed during the latter ten days of Ramadan known as *i'tikaf*. Certain conditions apply to *i'tikaf* itself, such as not leaving the mosque unless it is absolutely necessary, and not engaging in sexual intercourse. Of course, retreats may be embarked on throughout the month as the person pleases, or in as much as he or she is able.

## FASTING AS AN EXPIATION

In certain situations fasting may be resorted to as a compensation for wrong actions, or for the omission of action or for the inability to perform actions.

### i - For oaths

> Allah does not call you to account for what is vain in your oaths, but He does call you to account for making deliberate oaths. The expiation is the feeding of ten poor men out of the customary food you feed your families with, or their clothing, or the freeing of a slave; but whoever cannot find the means then fasting for three days. This is the expiation of your oaths. Thus does Allah make clear to you His communications that you may be grateful. (5:89)

The circumstances which brought about the revelation of this verse involved a Muslim man, 'Abdullah ibn Rawahah, who swore at his wife out of anger that he would not touch her food. He later broke his oath, however, in order to please a house-guest, since it is a recommended action to break a voluntary or expiatory fast if one has guests, so that they may feel at ease. Informed of what happened, the Prophet told 'Abdullah that he had done well. Most scholars and commentators say that no expiation is necessary for such foolish oaths.

There are three types of oaths. The first kind upholds a lawful action, such as, 'I swear by Allah that I will not drink alcohol'. If such an oath were to be broken one would clearly be going against a Divine command and thereby committing a wrong action. Breaking such an oath requires that it be expiated.

The second kind if upheld would be committing a wrong action and by breaking that oath one is reverting to correct action, such as, 'I swear by Allah that I will not pray'. No expiation is required for breaking such an oath.

The third type of oath is frivolous and may be kept or broken without expiation, such as 'I swear by Allah that I will not wear these clothes'.

## ii - For the compensation of certain Pilgrimage rites

And accomplish the pilgrimage and the visit for Allah but if you are prevented, (send) whatever offering is easy to obtain, and do not shave your heads until the offering reaches its destination; but whoso among you is sick or has an ailment of the head, he [should effect] a compensation by fasting or alms or sacrificing; then when you are secure, whoever profits by combining the visit with the pilgrimage [should take] whatever offering is easy to obtain; but he who cannot find [any offering] should fast for three days during the pilgrimage and for seven days upon [his] return; these [make] ten [days] complete; this is for one whose family is not present in the Sacred Mosque. Be careful [of your duty] to Allah and know that Allah is severe in requiting [evil]. (2:196)

## iii - For accidentally killing a believer

And it does not behove a believer to kill a believer save by mistake, and whoever kills a believer by mistake he should free a believing slave, and blood-money should be paid to [the deceased's] people unless they remit it as alms. But if he be from a tribe hostile to you and he is a believer, the freeing of a believing slave [suffices]; and if he be from a tribe between whom and you there is a covenant, the blood-money should be paid to his people along with the freeing of a believing slave. But he who cannot find [a slave] should fast for two months successively: a penance from Allah, and Allah is ever Knowing, Wise. (4:92)

This verse was revealed after Abu al-Darda' and members of a raiding party killed a suspected bandit whilst the victim called out 'There is no God but Allah!' The incident troubled him, so he informed the Prophet of what he had done. The Prophet said: 'Did you open his heart to disclose the truth of what he said? He told you with his tongue, but you did not believe him.' Thus did the Prophet reprimand Abu al-Darda' for killing a person who had outwardly expressed his faith (Islam). One has to accept in good faith people's words and let their actions later be their judge.

### iv - For killing game while on Pilgrimage

O you who believe! do not kill while you are on pilgrimage. Whoever among you kills it intentionally the compensation thereof is the like of what he killed, from the cattle, as two just persons among you shall judge, as an offering to be brought to the Ka'bah, or the expiation thereof is the feeding of the poor or the equivalent in fasting, that he may taste the consequence of his heinous deed. Allah has pardoned what is gone by. Whoever returns (to it), Allah will exact retribution from him; and Allah is Mighty, the Lord of Retribution. (5:95)

The prohibition on killing game during the pilgrimage is a symbol of respect for the security of the Ka'bah; it is also to protect the animal species and a rule of safety for the large number of people gathering for the pilgrimage. Fasting is one way of expiating any violation of this injunction.

### v - For an ancient Arab custom

[As for] those of you who put away their wives by likening (comparing) their backs to their mothers they are not their mothers. Their mothers are none other thatn those who gave them birth. Most surely they utter a hateful word and a falsehood, and most surely Allah is Pardoning, Forgiving.

And [as for] those who put away their wives by likening their backs to the backs of their mothers, then would recall what they said, they should free a captive before they touch each other; so that you are admonished. And Allah is aware of what you do.

But whoever has not the means let him fast for two months successively before they touch each other. Then he who is not able let him feed sixty needy ones in order that you may have faith in Allah and His Messenger. These are Allah's limits, and the unbelievers shall have a painful punishment. (58:2-4)

In pre-Islamic Arabia if a husband were to say to his wife, 'You are to me as the back of my mother', it would be the equivalent of a divorce, the difference being that the woman was not free to leave her husband's house and marry someone else. She had to remain in the house as a discarded wife.

The specific occasion for the revelation of this verse was when a man called 'Aws Ibn Samit came to regret having uttered this phrase to his wife and thereby rendered her forbidden to him. His wife Khawlah went to the Prophet to seek advice and said to him, 'O Messenger of Allah, by Him Who revealed to you the Book, he (i.e. 'Aws) did not mention divorce and he is the father of my children and the most beloved of people to me.' Then she cried out to Allah in despair, 'O Lord, send down your revelation [concerning the matter] on the tongue of Your Prophet.' Thus did this revelation put an end to this misguided custom.

# Chapter Four

## Selected Traditions on Fasting

While the Qur'an is founded on revealed truth, the Prophetic practices, actions, and sayings (*sunnah*) are its complement. Thus, after the Qur'an the next source of knowledge and practice in Islam is the Prophetic way and conduct. Knowledge of the Prophet's way is obtained from the corpus of narratives that relate to his deeds and sayings, commonly referred to as 'traditions' (*ahadith*; singular: *hadith,* though the latter is used collectively).

After the Prophet Muhammad's death two main streams of thought developed regarding traditions and religious elaboration. The fundamental difference between these two streams was that one believed Imam 'Ali ibn Abi Talib to have been appointed by the Prophet as his successor. This became known as the Shi'a (followers) of 'Ali, and later became known as the Ja'fari or Imami School of Law. The traditions and teachings of this stream is based on what came through the teaching of Imam 'Ali and the successive eleven Imams, all of whom were confirmed as rightful spiritual leaders as descendants of the Prophet.

The second stream takes its traditions from the great companions and the caliphs who succeeded the Prophet – Abu Bakr, 'Umar, and 'Uthman. This is the Sunni majority which settled some two centuries later into four main Sunni Schools of thought, the Maliki, Shafi'i, Hanafi and Hanbali.

To ensure the authenticity of the Prophetic traditions a system of scholarship evolved to categorize them and establish their chains of transmission. Among the Sunni majority the growth of this science culminated in six major compendiums, commonly referred to as 'The Accurate Six' (*Al-Ashah al-Sittah*). The *Sahih* (singular of *Ashah*) of Bukhari and the *Sahih* of Muslim are the two most often quoted sources. Among the Shi'ites, four major collections are usually referred to as *Al-Kutub al-Arba'a* – 'The Four (original) Books'.

This chapter on the traditions of fasting will draw mostly on the chains of transmission through the Prophet's Household, the Ahl al-Bayt, as narrated by Imam Ja'far al-Sadiq (83-148 Hijri). During his lifetime he was the most widely acknowledged spiritual master of Muslims. The chain of narration from the Imams links directly to the Prophet himself and is therefore considered most reliable in all aspects.

# PART I

## A – The Reason, Benefit and Virtues of Fasting

1.  The Prophet said:

    For everything there is a door, and the door of worship is fasting.

2.  The Prophet said to his companions:

    Shall I inform you of something which will keep the Shaytan away from you as far as the East is from the West?

    They said: Yes, please tell us, O Prophet of Allah.

    He said:

    Fasting: it will blacken his face;

    Charity: it will break his back;

    Love of Allah and assisting in good deeds: it will break his strength.

    For everything there is a way of purification, and for the body it is fasting.

3.  The Prophet also said:

Allah the Exalted and all the angels are praying for those who fast.

4. Imam al-Sadiq was asked about the reason for fasting and he replied:

Allah made fasting obligatory in order to equalize the rich and the poor. By experiencing hunger, the rich have more compassion for the poor. The rich would never experience hunger for they are able to provide whatever they wish for themselves.

5. Imam al-Rida said:

By the experience of hunger and thirst the slave of Allah may become submissive, surrendered, patient and rewarded. The fast is an indication to him of how intense the breaking of desires is in the Hereafter, of the temporality of worldly existence, as well as an indication of death. One who fasts obtains knowledge of the state of need and utter poverty of people in this life and the next.

6. Imam al-Rida received a letter asking him about the reason for fasting and he responded by saying:

The reason for fasting is that man may know the pain and discomfort of hunger and thirst in order that he become fearful, humble, submissive and patient with what befalls him. Restraint from desires has its recompense. Also, the one who fasts becomes aware of the intensity of poverty which those who have no means may feel; thus he is more willing to give of his wealth, particularly what is made obligatory by Divine Law. Fasting has been prescribed in the month of Ramadan because in this month Allah revealed the Qur'an to the Prophet Muhammad. In this month, as well, is the Night of Determination or Decree.

7. Imam 'Ali said:

A group of Jews came to the Messenger of Allah and the most knowledgeable among them asked him questions. Among these questions was: "For what reason did Allah enjoin fasting for thirty days upon your community?" The Messenger of Allah responded saying: "When Adam ate

33

from the tree the food remained in his stomach for thirty days, so Allah enjoined thirty days of hunger and thirst upon his descendants. He granted them the favour of eating at night. As He enjoined upon Adam so He enjoined upon my nation." Then the Prophet recited the following verse of the Qur'an: "Fasting is prescribed for you as it was prescribed for those before you for a certain number of days that perhaps you may be cautiously aware". The Jew said: "You have spoken the truth, Muhammad. What then is the reward of one who fasts Ramadan?" The Prophet replied: "Allah is obliged to grant the believer who fasts contentedly in Ramadan seven things:

The first is that what is forbidden is dissolved from his body. The second is that he comes close to Allah's mercy. Third, the sins of his father Adam will have been forgiven. The fourth is that Allah will ease the throes of death for him. The fifth is security from hunger and thirst on the Day of Resurrection. The sixth is that Allah will grant him freedom from the Fire. And the seventh is that Allah will feed him from the bounties of the Garden."

The Jew said: "You have spoken the truth, Muhammad."

8. The Messenger also said:

Whoever fasts Ramadan, guards his private parts and his tongue and restrains himself from injury to other people has been forgiven by Allah for his mistakes, past and future. Allah has freed him from the Fire, caused him to occupy the permanent abode, and accepted his intercession for as many of those who have committed wrong actions amongst the people of belief and unity as there are grains of sand in 'Alij [a place in the desert of Arabia].

9. Imam al-Sadiq said:

Allah, the Glorious and Mighty, entrusts one who fasts for Him in the discomfort of heat, stricken by thirst, with a thousand angels to wipe his face and give him good tidings until he breaks his fast. At this point Allah says: "How sweet is your odour and your soul! O angels, witness that I have forgiven him".

10. He also said:

> When a severe accident befalls a person they should fast. Surely Allah has said: "Seek help in patience and prayer".

11. Allah, the Exalted, said (in the words of His Prophet):

> Every action of a son of Adam is his, except fasting. It is Mine and I reward it. Fasting is a protection for the believing slave on the Day of Reckoning just as one's weapons protect one in the world. The breath of one who fasts smells better to Allah than the aroma of musk. The one who fasts rejoices over two things: the time of breaking the fast when he may eat and drink, and the time when he meets Me, for I cause him to enter the Garden.

## B - The Prophet's Injunction Concerning Ramadan

1. The Messenger of Allah addressed the people one day saying:

> Allah's month has approached with blessings, mercy, and forgiveness. It is the best of months in the sight of Allah, its days are the best of days, its nights the best of nights, and its hours the best of hours. During this month you are summoned to Allah's hospitality. You become the people of esteem and respect in Allah's sight. In this month your breaths are glorification of Allah and your sleep is worship. Your actions are accepted and what you ask for is answered, so beseech Allah, your Lord, with sincere intention and a purified heart that He may grant you success in your fast and recitation of His Book. How unhappy is the one whom Allah has banished from His forgiveness in this great month. Remember when you are hungry and thirsty the hunger and thirst of the Day of Reckoning. Give charity to those in need and those stricken with poverty among you. Act in a dignified manner to the great ones among you. Have mercy for the young ones, pray for your relatives and restrain your speech. Lower your gaze from what is not permissible to be seen and avert your ears from what is not permissible to be heard. Have compassion for orphans as you would like people to have compassion for your children if they were orphaned. Turn away from your wrong actions to Allah and raise your hands to Him in supplication during the times of

prayer, for they are the best of times in which Allah looks upon His slaves with mercy. He answers them when they ask Him in need, responding to their cries and supplication, giving them when they ask (Him).

O People, most surely your souls are taken as security for your actions, so redeem them by asking for forgiveness. Your backs are heavy with burdens, so lighten them with long prostrations. Know that Allah has sworn by His might that He will not punish the one who prays and performs prostration, and that He will not frighten them with the Fire on the day mankind stands before the Lord of the Worlds.

O people, whoever gives food to a believer who is fasting in order that he may break his fast in this month has the [same] reward as that of one who has freed a soul, in addition to forgiveness for his wrong past actions.

Someone then asked him:

O Messenger of Allah, what if we are not able to do that?

He replied:

Fear the Fire even if by half a date. Fear the Fire even if by a drink of water. Whoever perfects his behaviour in this month will have permission to cross the Bridge on the day when feet will slip. Whoever lightens the burden of the ones whom his right hand possesses will find that Allah lightens his accountability. Whoever refrains from wrongdoing where they are concerned Allah will restrain His anger on the day he meets Him. Whoever is generous to an orphan will find Allah generous to him on the day he meets Him. Whoever cuts off his mercy to an orphan will find that Allah cut him off from His mercy on the day of meeting. Whoever prays supererogatory prayers in this month, Allah will free him from the Fire. Whoever performs obligatory actions has the reward of seventy obligatory actions in other months. Whoever increases his prayer upon me, Allah will increase the weight of his scale on the day when the scales are lightened. Whoever recites a verse of the Qur'an in this month has the reward of completing [a reading of] the Qur'an in other months.

O people, the doors of the Garden are open in this month so ask your Lord not to close them to you. The doors of the Fire are shut, so ask your Lord not to allow them to open for you. Those who are evil are chained, so ask your Lord not to allow them to have any power over you.

Thereupon Imam 'Ali stood up and asked:

O Messenger of Allah, what acts are of the most merit in this month?

He answered:

O Abu'l-Hasan, the most meritorious acts in this month are scrupulousness in avoiding whatever is forbidden by Allah and whatever is reprehensible.

## C - The Intention to Fast

1. Imam 'Ali said:

   When a man has not previously made an intention to fast (voluntarily) then makes the intention to fast before eating or drinking that day he has the choice of fasting [i.e. he can do so].

2. Imam Musa ibn Ja'far was asked whether someone should fast on a day when they awaken after daybreak during the month of Ramadan and has not eaten, drunk or made the intention to fast after daylight has spread ['after daylight has spread' refers to the time between daybreak and the descent of the sun from its zenith]. The Imam replied:

   Yes, he should fast and regard it as fulfilment of the obligation of that obligatory day of Ramadan.

3. Imam al-Sadiq was asked:

   Is it permissible for a man who must make up a fast of Ramadan to do so on a day when he awakens and by the time of the afternoon prayer has not yet made the intention to fast but has not yet eaten?

The Imam replied in the affirmative. It is recommended, however, that the intention to fast be made at the beginning of the time for the afternoon prayer, which is after the descent of the sun from its zenith.

## D - Fasting the Day of Doubt

The Day of Doubt, as it is known, is when one cannot be sure whether it is the last day of Sha'ban (the month preceding Ramadan) or the first day of Ramadan.

1. Imam al-Sadiq was asked about fasting on the Day of Doubt and gave this answer:

    Fast on this day. If it still be Sha'ban, the fast will be voluntary and if it be Ramadan you will have been fortunate to have accomplished the fast.

2. Imam 'Ali ibn al-Husayn said:

    We have been enjoined to fast the Day of Doubt as a day of Sha'ban, and not as a day of Ramadan without sighting the moon.

If it subsequently transpires that the day was in fact Ramadan, Then the intention automatically transfers to Ramadan and the fast is accepted as the fast of Ramadan.

3. Imam 'Ali said:

    It is better that I fast a day of Sha'ban than miss a day of Ramadan.

In other words, if one does not fast the day of doubt and finds out later that it was the first day of Ramadan, he will have missed the fast of that day.

## E - Beginning and Ending the Fast of Ramadan

1. Imam al-Rida said:

    Fasting begins when the new moon of Ramadan is sighted and is broken when the new moon of Shawwal is sighted.

38

2. Imam al-Sadiq said:

> Fast upon sighting the new moon of Ramadan, and break the fast upon sighting the new moon of Shawwal, even if only two honest and upright witnesses among you see it.

3. Imam Musa ibn Ja'far was asked if one should fast upon seeing the new moon if no one else does so. He said:

> If he has no doubt about it, he alone should fast; otherwise he should fast with the people when they fast.

4. Imam al-Sadiq said:

> The fast of Ramadan begins by sighting the moon, not by opinion, idea or supposition. Ramadan is sometimes 29 days and sometimes 30.

5. A man asked him about sighting the new moon of Ramadan when the horizon was obscured by clouds on the 29th of Sha'ban. The Imam said:

> Do not fast Ramadan unless you see the moon. If another town or city testify that they have seen it, then fast. If you see it in the middle of the day, then complete the fast for the rest of the day.

6. He also said:

> If the new moon is seen during the day, before the sun reaches its zenith, then it belongs to the night before and if after the zenith then to the coming night.

7. Imam 'Ali said:

> It is not permissible to accept the testimony of women concerning the new moon nor that of less than two men known for their honesty and uprightness.

8. Imam al-Baqir said:

> Fast when the people fast, and break the fast when they break it, for Allah has made appointed times for the new moons.

9. Imam al-Sadiq was approached concerning the sighting of the moon on the second night of the month and not the first and

was asked if it should be considered the second night even though the moon could not be sighted the night before, he replied in the affirmative. The inference here is that the first day of Ramadan must be made up after the Eid.

10. He also said:

> When the new moon of the month of Rajab appears, count 59 days then fast.

## F - Worship during Ramadan

1.  During the last Friday prayer of Sha'ban the Prophet addressed the congregation:

> A month has come to you within which is a night that is better than a thousand months. This month is Ramadan. Allah has enjoined fasting in it and prescribed rising in the night for prayer and remembrance. Supererogatory prayer during these nights is like 70 supererogatory prayers during the nights of other months. Allah bestows characteristics of excellence and piety, like the virtue of performing obligatory actions, upon whomever performs supererogatory prayers during the nights of Ramadan. Whoever performs obligatory actions in Ramadan enjoys the reward of one who has performed 70 obligatory action in other months.

> Ramadan is the month of patience, and the reward of patience is the garden. Ramadan is the month of consolation and charity. In it Allah increases the provisions of the believer. Whoever provides a believer with food so that he may break his fast receives from Allah the same reward as for freeing a slave and forgiveness for his wrong actions. Whoever alleviates the distress of an enslaved person will find that Allah lightens his accountability. The beginning of Ramadan is mercy, its middle is forgiveness and its end is the granting of requests and remission from the Fire. Four things may not be dispensed with during Ramadan: two of them are pleasing to Allah and two are indispensable. The two which please Allah are witnessing that there is no God except Allah and that Muhammad is His Messenger. As for the other two which should not be dispensed with, they are beseeching

Allah for one's needs and the Garden and seeking forgiveness and protection from the Fire.

2. Imam 'Ali said:

   During the month of Ramadan you must ask Allah's forgiveness and call on Him frequently. Calling on Allah eliminates afflictions and asking His forgiveness erases wrong actions.

3. He also said:

   When Ramadan began, the Messenger of Allah used to release every prisoner and he gave everyone what they asked of him.

4. Imam al-Sadiq said:

   The months with Allah are twelve in the Book of Allah since He created the heavens and the earth. The most honoured of the months is Ramadan, and the heart of Ramadan is the Night of Determination in which the Qur'an descended, so greet the month with the recitation of the Qur'an.

5. A man wrote to Imam 'Ali ibn al-Husayn, asking him about the ritual bath (*ghusl*) during the month of Ramadan, and the Imam replied:

   If you are able to bathe on the nights of the 17th, 19th, 21st and 23rd, then do so and formulate the intention for the Night of Determination. If you are not able to enliven yourself to this extent, then do not let the night of the 23rd escape you. Pray 100 cycles (*rak'at*), reciting in each the Fatihah once and Surah Ikhlas ten times.

6. Imam al-Sadiq said:

   Whoever reads the two chapters in the Qur'an of al-'Ankabut (The Spider) and al-Rum (The Romans) on the 23rd night of the month of Ramadan is among the people of the Garden, not to be excluded from it.

7. Imam al-Sadiq said:

   Upon sighting the new moon of Ramadan the Messenger of Allah used to face the Ka'bah, raise his hands and say: "O

Lord, allow it (i.e. the moon) to shine upon us with protection and faith, flawlessness and submission, dignified well-being, ample provision and resistance to illness. O Lord, bestow upon us the fast of Ramadan that we may stand in prayer during its nights and recite the Qur'an. O Lord, grant us surrender and take over the management of our affairs in it, protect us and grant us salvation."

## G - Divine Revelation during Ramadan

Imam al-Sadiq said:

The Torah was revealed on the sixth day of the month of Ramadan, the Gospel was revealed on the twelfth day of the month of Ramadan, and the Psalms were revealed on the eighteenth day. The Qur'an was revealed on the Night of Determination.

## H - Ramadan – One of the Names of Allah

While Imam al-Sadiq was with a group of men Ramadan was mentioned and he said:

Do not say this is Ramadan, for Ramadan has not left and has not come. Ramadan is one of Allah's names, Mighty and Majestic is He, and He does not come and go, for only the transitory does so. Rather, say the month of Ramadan. This month of Ramadan is the one in which the Qur'an was revealed. Allah made it an example, a promise and a warning.

## I - Making up the Fast

1. When Imam al-Sadiq was asked about one who is sick during the month of Ramadan and cannot fast and does not recover until the following Ramadan, he answered:

He should give charity for the first Ramadan and fast the second. If he recovered after the first Ramadan and did not fast until reaching the second, he should fast that Ramadan, plus another month, and give charity also.

2. Imam al-Sadiq said:

> Whoever breaks the fast of Ramadan with a valid excuse and reaches the next Ramadan having been sick and unable to make up what he missed, let him give charity for each day he missed of one *mudd* (equivalent to a meal or about 750 grams of grain). As for myself, I fast and give charity.

3. He also said:

> Whoever breaks the fast of Ramadan with a valid excuse and makes up what he has missed by fasting consecutive days, this is best. It is, however, permissible for one to break up the days.

4. Imam al-Rida stated:

> Fasting is the Garden, and charity erases wrong actions.

## J - Retreat (*i'tikaf*) in the Mosque during Ramadan

1. Imam al-Sadiq said:

> One may not go into retreat (*i'tikaf*) in a mosque unless it is during the last ten days of Ramadan.

2. He also said:

> Withdrawal into a mosque can only be done while fasting.

3. And:

> The one who secludes himself in a mosque should do so in the central mosque where the Friday prayer is performed.

> One should not perform retreat in a mosque for less than three days.

4. Imam 'Ali was asked whether a man on retreat could enjoy sexual relations with his wife. He replied:

> He must not go into his wife by night or by day.

5. Imam al-Sadiq said:

> It is not proper for one who is on retreat in a mosque to go out of the mosque but for a pressing need, and then he must

not sit down until after he has returned. One should not leave [the mosque] except for a funeral or upon becoming ill; even then he should not sit until after he has returned. Retreat for women is the same.

6.   He also said:

When in retreat one should not sniff perfume or strong aromatic scents, he should not argue or oppose, nor should he engage in buying and selling.

## K - The Eid Festival after Ramadan

Imam al-Rida was asked why the day of the Eid was made a day of celebration, he responded thus:

In order that the Muslims gather together for Allah and praise Him for what He has bestowed upon them. Thus it is a day of celebration, a day of gathering, a day of breakfasting, a day of charity, a day of longing and a day of supplication. The Magnification (*takbir*) is repeated more in the festival prayer than in the other prayers because it is a glorification and exaltation of Allah and praise for His guidance and protection, as He said: "In order that you exalt Allah for His guidance – perhaps that you may be thankful".

# PART II

# CONDITIONS GOVERNING THE FAST

## L - Actions that break the Fast

### i.   *Lying*

Imam al-Sadiq said:

Lying [i.e. about Allah, the Prophet, or the Imams] nullifies ablution (*wudu'*) and breaks the fast of the one who is fasting.

## ii. Immersion in water

Imam al-Sadiq said:

> A man who is fasting may immerse himself in water but may not immerse his head.

## iii. Applying Antimony, taking snuff and cupping

Imam 'Ali said:

> The one who is fasting may put antimony in his eyes, but snuff is reprehensible (makruh).

Imam al-Sadiq confirms that it is permissible for one fasting to be cupped and to have oil poured in his ears (for treatment of earache). Imam 'Ali, however, is said to have disliked cupping because he feared that it may cause one who is fasting to faint, thereby obliging him to break his fast.

## iv. Intentionally breaking the fast

1. Imam al-Sadiq was asked about what one should do if he intentionally broke the fast of Ramadan for one day without an excuse. He said:

   > Free a person, fast two consecutive months, or feed sixty people. If he cannot do any one of these three things, then he should give charity as much as he is capable of giving.

2. A man came to the Prophet and said: I have intentionally committed a sin during the month of Ramadan while I was fasting.

   The Prophet then said to him: Free a slave.

   The man said: I cannot find the means.

   So the Prophet said: Fast two consecutive months.

   The man replied: I am not able to do this.

   The Prophet then said: Give charity to sixty poor people.

   The man said: I have not the means to do this either.

The Prophet then gave the man a large basket of dates and said to him: Take these dates and give them as charity.

The man said: I swear by Him Who brought you forth as a Prophet with the truth, I do not know of any people more in need than those in my own house.

The Prophet then said to him: Take this then and feed your family. The sin you have committed is expiated.

3.  Imam Musa ibn Ja'far was asked what is due from a man who marries a woman (i.e. has sexual intercourse) while he is fasting in Ramadan, and he answered:

    He must make up the day of fasting and free a slave. If he has not the means to free a slave, he must fast for two consecutive months; and if he cannot do this, he must feed sixty poor people. If he cannot do that, he should ask Allah's forgiveness.

### v.  *Inadvertently breaking the fast*

1.  Imam al-Sadiq was asked about one who forgets that he is fasting, eats, drinks and then remembers that he is fasting. The Imam responded:

    His fast is not broken, rather, Allah has bestowed sustenance upon him, so let him complete his fast.

2.  Imam al-Sadiq was also asked about someone who forgets he is fasting and has sexual relations with his wife. He said:

    His situation is the same as the one who inadvertently eats while fasting.

### vi.  *Concerning sexual matters in Ramadan*

1.  Imam al-Rida said that whoever has intercourse in daytime during Ramadan while fasting must make up the day and also offer something in expiation. Similarly, for each additional time he has sexual intercourse during the same day he must expiate his transgression in the same measure.

2. Imam al-Sadiq was queried about the situation of a man who has a wet dream and falls asleep before taking a ritual bath. He said it did not matter. Likewise, he was asked about a man who falls asleep after such a dream without performing the ritual purification bath (*ghusl*) and awakens after dawn. He said:

    No harm; he bathes, prays and fasts.

3. He was also asked what one should do if a man became ritually impure during Ramadan, sleeps and awakens, sleeps again and reawakens, sleeps a third time and then awakens after dawn. For this case he explained:

    He must fast that day and make up another day as well. If he had not awoken the second time before dawn, no compensatory fast would have been necessary.

4. As for someone who becomes ritually impure during Ramadan and intentionally neglects to perform the ritual purification until after dawn, he said:

    He must free a slave, fast two consecutive months or feed sixty poor people.

    Then he added:

    This is what is owing from him [by law], but I do not think he could ever recover what he lost by intentional neglect (even by the expiation).

5. In the case of someone who became impure in the night and forgot to purify himself until a week had passed or the remainder of the month of Ramadan, the Imam said:

    He must make up all his prayers and fasting.

6. Imam al-Sadiq said:

    Kissing [i.e. simple kissing] does not invalidate the fast.

7. Imam 'Ali advised:

    If one of you cannot remain patient until nightfall he should remember the saying: "The fight begins with only so much as a slap". If a man lies with his wife during Ramadan [without having intercourse] and ejaculates, he must free a slave.

## M - Further Conditions to be Observed when Fasting

### i. Rinsing the mouth and nostrils

1. When asked about the permissibility of rinsing the mouth and nose during the ablution for prayer during Ramadan, Imam al-Sadiq said:

   You may do so, but do not overdo it.

2. Regarding rinsing the mouth he also said by way of caution:

   One should not swallow his saliva until he has spat three times.

### ii. Scents

Imam al-Sadiq refrained from smelling sweet basil while fasting. When asked about this practice he said:

I dislike mixing my fast with sensual pleasure.

On one particular day when the Persians used to fast, they would smell narcissus in order to eliminate thirst. This practice became a regular tradition and because of that this practice became prohibited for Muslims, although scent as such does not nullify the fast.

### iii. Tasting dishes while cooking and swallowing phlegm

1. Imam al-Sadiq said:

   There is no objection for one who is fasting to taste what is in the pot (whilst cooking).

2. Regarding phlegm:

   There is no objection to swallowing it if one is fasting.

### iv. Beginning the fast at dawn

1. Imam Musa ibn Ja'far was asked about what should be done if a man drank after dawn, not knowing that dawn has occurred. He replied:

   He should fast [the remainder of] the day and perform a compensatory fast for that day as well. If the day [on which this happens] is a compensatory fast for Ramadan in some other month, then his fast is broken and he should perform it another day.

2. Imam al-Sadiq said:

   Eat only up to the point that you have no doubt that dawn has not yet occurred.

### v. Breaking the fast at sunset

1. The Prophet said to 'Ali:

   O 'Ali, the believer has three joys in this world: meeting his brothers, breaking the fast and keeping vigil toward the end of night in prayer.

2. Imam al-Sadiq said:

   Whoever broke the fast before nightfall, without attaining certainty that the sun had set, must compensate for it.

3. When asked about a man who, after making enquiries, thought that the sun had set and then broke his fast, and who then saw the sun still up, Imam al-Sadiq said:

   He does not (need to) repeat the fast.

The difference between this situation and the preceding one is that in this case the man had done all he could to be certain that the sun had set, whereas in the previous case proper investigation had not been made to attain certainty.

4. Imam al-Sadiq said:

   When the sun disappears, breaking the fast is permissible and the prayer becomes obligatory. The beginning of night is when the sun's disk has disappeared below the horizon. The sign that indicates with certainty that the sun had gone down is the absence of red in the Eastern sky [as a safe precaution, several minutes after sunset].

## vi. Praying the sunset prayer before breaking the fast

1.  When asked about praying the sunset prayer (*maghrib*) before breaking the fast, Imam al-Sadiq said:

    Two obligatory acts are demanded at the same time: the prayer and breaking the fast. Thus, begin with the better of the two, and this is prayer.

2.  When someone asked him whether he should fast first or pray, he answered:

    If a person has people with him who fear delaying their supper, then let him eat with them, but if not, let him pray and then break fast.

3.  He had also said:

    Precede the breaking of the fast with the prayer unless you are with people who break their fast first. Do not make your action incompatible with what they do; rather, break fast with them. Otherwise, perform the prayer first – it is better than breaking fast, for your prayer will be written for you while you are fasting, and this is more desirable.

## vii. Feeding the fasting

1.  The Prophet said:

    He who gives food to someone so that they may break their fast has the same reward of fasting of the one whom he has fed, without diminishment, as well as the reward of the good actions that they perform by means of the strength they acquire from the food.

2. He also said:

> The one who provides food for the breaking of the fast of a believer reaps the reward from Allah of one who frees a slave as well as forgiveness for his past wrong actions.

### viii. The pre-dawn meal (suhur) and the midday nap

1. The Prophet said:

> The early morning meal before dawn is a blessing.

2. He also said:

> Take the early morning meal even if it is just a mouthful of water, for the blessings of Allah are upon those who do so.

3. And:

> Eat the early morning meal for the fast of the day and take a midday nap for standing up in the night in prayer.

### ix. Foods for breaking the fast

1. Imam al-Sadiq said:

> The Prophet used to break his fast on two things: dates and water, or raisins and water. He used to eat these two for the early morning meal as well.

2. He also said:

> Qanbar, the companion of Imam 'Ali, came to him with barley and date-paste for the Imam to break fast with. Before Imam 'Ali took the food he said: "In the name of Allah. Our Lord, for you we have fasted and upon Your provision we break the fast, so accept it from us, for surely You are the One Who hears and knows".

3. Imam al-Sadiq said:

> The Messenger of Allah broke his fast on fresh dates when they were in season and on dry dates when fresh ones were out of season.

4. He also said:

> Imam 'Ali preferred to break the fast on milk.

### x.  *Breaking the voluntary fast if offered food*

1. Several of the Imams have said that:

> Whoever enters the house of his brother while fasting and breaks his fast has two rewards: the reward of his intention to fast, and the reward of bringing his brother joy [by his visit].

2. Imam al-Sadiq said:

> Break your fast for your brother Muslim, for the joy you bring him is a greater reward than your fast.

# PART III

## N - The Inner Conditions of Fasting

1. The Messenger of Allah said:

> There is no slave who wakes up while fasting, is insulted by someone and says [in response], "I am fasting, peace be upon you", but that the Lord says: "My slave seeks protection by fasting against another of My slaves. I grant him protection from My Fire and cause him to enter My Garden."

2. Imam al-Sadiq said:

> When you fast, let your ears, eyes, hair, skin and other senses fast, and do not allow your day of fasting to be like other days.

3. He also said:

> Fasting is not from food and drink alone. Maryam said: "I have made a vow to the Merciful to fast", that is, to abstain from speech. Thus when you fast, guard your tongue, lower your eyes and do not dispute or be envious. The Messenger

of Allah heard a woman insult her neighbour while she was fasting, so he called for food, gave it to her and ordered her to eat. She said: "I am fasting!" He said: "How can you be fasting while you have insulted your neighbour? Fasting is not from food and drink alone." So when you fast, your ears and eyes should abstain from what is base and forbidden, from contemptuously rebuffing others and from injuring those who serve you. You must adorn yourself with the dignity of one who is fasting. Do not make a day of fasting the same as other days.

4. And:

Fasting is not from food and drink alone; rather, it has a condition which must be sustained until the fast is completed, and that is inner silence. As for listening to speech, Maryam, the daughter of 'Imran, said: "I have made a vow to the Merciful to fast, so I may not speak to anyone today", meaning [she was observing] silence. When you fast, guard your tongues from speaking falsely and deceitfully, lower you eyes, refrain from controversy, envy and slander, do not be indecisive or lie, refrain from sensual contact, do not participate in situations of conflict or anger, do not insult, curse, scold or abuse anyone, do not shout, yell, or argue, do not waste or squander, do not oppress anyone, do not act foolishly or drive anyone away, and do not become neglectful of remembering Allah and prayer. Adhere to silence, tranquillity, forbearance, patience, truthfulness, avoidance of bad company, dishonest speech, and evil thoughts.

Elevate yourself to the state of the Hereafter, waiting expectantly for your fate, for what Allah has promised you, prepared for the encounter with Him. You must have tranquillity, dignity, submissiveness, obedience, humility and the abasement of the slave fearing his master with hope and fear, desire and dread.

You must purify your heart of faults, purify your innermost self from guile and deceit, and cleanse your physical form of filth and moral defilement, becoming free of whatever stands in your way to Allah. You must draw near to Allah during your fast by silence in every situation from what Allah has prohibited, secretly and openly. You must fear Allah as He ought to be feared, overtly and covertly, and give yourself up to Allah during the days of your fast. You must empty your heart and prepare it for Him by what He has commanded for you and invoke Him.

When you have done all of this then you are fasting for Allah, covertly as He has commanded. Anything less than that diminishes the extent of this fast, for the fast is not just from eating or drinking. Allah has made abstention from eating and drinking a means by which one may refrain from detestable actions and speech. How many a fast is broken by little of the correct condition of fasting even though there is much hunger?

## O - Fasting while Travelling or Unwell

1.  The Prophet said:

    Allah, the Mighty, the Majestic, has given charity to travellers and those who are sick among my community by allowing them to shorten their prayers and break their fast. Is there anyone among you who would return Allah's charity?

2.  He also said:

    Allah, the Mighty, the Majestic, bestowed a gift upon me and my nation: He has granted us generosity not given to other nations; [it is] breaking the fast and shortening the prayer while travelling. Whoever does not do this has returned Allah's gift.

3.  Imam 'Ali ibn al-Husayn stated that:

    There exists a difference of opinion among the public as to whether one should fast while travelling or ill. Some say one should fast, others say no, and still others say one may fast if one wishes and refrain from fasting if one wishes. As for us, we say that if one is on a journey or ill, he must compensate for the [missed] fast at another time, for Allah, the Mighty, the Majestic, says: "Whoever among you is sick or on a journey so [let him fast] a number of other days".

4. Imam al-Sadiq said:

> When a person travels during the month of Ramadan, he should break his fast. The Messenger of Allah left Madinah for Makkah during the month of Ramadan with a group of people. Between the afternoon and late afternoon prayer the Prophet ate from a leg of [roast] sheep and called for a bowl of water from which he drank. Thus did he break his fast. The people broke their fast with him, except for some who completed their fast. Those he called disobedient.

5. Imam 'Ali ibn al-Husayn said:

> There is no righteousness in fasting while on a journey.

6. A man asked Imam al-Sadiq what one who fasted while travelling should do. The Imam replied:

> If he had been informed that the Prophet had prohibited such an action, then he must compensate for the fast later on, and if he had not been informed, then nothing is expected of him.

7. Imam al-Sadiq said:

> When the month of Ramadan comes, Allah has established a condition for it, as He stated: "Whoever among you witnesses the month, let him fast". When Ramadan begins no one should go out unless to begin his journey for the Lesser Pilgrimage, or because he fears damage to his wealth, or to help a brother for whom he fears ruin. He should never go out to destroy the wealth of his brother Muslim. After 23 nights of Ramadan have passed, he may go out wherever he wishes.

8. Imam al-Sadiq was also asked about a man who leaves his house, wishing to travel while he is still fasting, to which he replied:

> If he goes out before half the day has passed, he should break his fast and make up for it later, but if he goes out after the sun has reached its zenith, he should complete his fast.

9. When asked what a traveller should do about his fast upon approaching his place of residence during Ramadan at the time of daybreak. He said:

> If dawn had come and he had still not arrived, he has a choice: he may fast, and if he wishes he may break his fast.

10. The Imam was once asked what should a traveller do if he returns home on a day in Ramadan during which he has eaten before his arrival. He said:

> He should refrain from eating for the remainder of the day and compensate for it later.

11. Imam Musa ibn Ja'far was asked whether a person who travels during Ramadan and remains in a place for several days should fast. He replied:

> Not unless he has decided to remain in the place for ten days (or more). Should he do so, he should fast and pray the regular prayer.

12. Imam al-Sadiq was asked what a man should do if he had taken an oath to fast but wished to go on pilgrimage (i.e. the lesser pilgrimage: *'umrah*). He replied:

> He should go and not fast while on the road, then when he returns he should make up what he has missed.

13. He was also asked whether a man should fast if, having vowed to Allah to fast a specific amount of time, then something occurs which makes it necessary for him to travel. He said:

> When travelling he should not fast because neither an obligatory nor a voluntary fast is permissible while travelling. Fasting during travel is an act of disobedience.

A companion of Imam al-Sadiq asked him about fasting while travelling and he said:

> There is no fasting while on a journey. People have fasted while having knowledge of what the Messenger of Allah enjoined, and he called them disobedient. There is no fasting

during a journey except the three days which Allah had enjoined during the Hajj Pilgrimage.*

14. Imam al-Sadiq said:

The Messenger of Allah did not fast voluntarily or obligatorily while travelling.

15. When Imam 'Ali was asked about the permissibility of having sexual intercourse with one's wife during daytime while travelling in Ramadan, he said:

There is no objection.

16. And Imam al-Sadiq said:

Allah has authorized breaking the fast and shortening the prayer for one who is travelling. The traveller is required to make up what he has missed of fasting at another time, but he is not required to make up what he has left out of prayers.

17. Imam al-Sadiq said that a man came to the Prophet and asked:

O Messenger of Allah, shall I fast the month of Ramadan while travelling?

The Prophet replied:

No.

Then the man asked:

Should I then travel?

The Prophet said:

Surely Allah has been charitable to those among my nation who are sick or travelling, allowing them to break the fast of Ramadan. Would you not be astonished at one who was reluctant to accept this charity, not wanting to accept Allah's favour upon him?

---

* Which is the compensation for omitting the sacrifice; fasting three days in Makkah and seven days upon returning home – obligatory for those living outside the environs of Makkah.

18. Imam 'Ali ibn al-Husayn said:

> If a traveller has eaten in the beginning of the day, then arrives home, he is instructed to abstain for the rest of the day. This is not an obligatory act, but rather, a courtesy.

## P - When to Resume Fasting after Illness

1.  A man asked Imam al-Sadiq:

> What point of recuperation must one who was sick reach in order to fast?

He replied:

> The person who is sick knows best when he is strong enough. When he reaches this point, let him fast.

2.  A man wrote to the same Imam asking precisely how ill a person must be to forego fasting or to sit while praying instead of standing. He replied:

> Man is a witness over himself.

Then he added:

> He must determine for he best knows himself.

## Q - Inability to Fast

1.  Imam al-Sadiq was asked about an old man too weak to fast the month of Ramadan. He said:

> For every day he should give alms to feed the poor in an appropriate amount.

2.  He was asked about Allah's words: 'And upon those who are capable [there devolves] a redemption by feeding the poor'.

He said:

> These are the elderly and sick who are not able to fast, and the women who fear for their children and the elderly.

3.  He was asked what one should do if he were afflicted by thirst to such an extent that he feared for his life. He said:

He should drink just enough to allay death, but not so much as to quench his thirst.

4. He also said:

The pregnant woman who is approaching delivery and the nursing mother with little milk may break their fast in the month of Ramadan if necessary. For every day they do not fast they must give alms of one *mudd* (about 750 grams of grain) and make up the fast later.

5. A man was feverish in Madinah one day during the month of Ramadan and Imam al-Sadiq sent him a bowl of vinegar and oil, with the message, 'Break your fast, for you are disabled'.

## R - Losing Consciousness for One Day or More

A man wrote to Imam al-Naqi asking if it were necessary for one who had lost consciousness for a day or more to make up his fast. He wrote back saying:

He does not need to make up his fast.

## S - Menstruation and Fasting

1. Imam al-Sadiq was asked if a fasting woman should break her fast if she began to menstruate in the daytime or in the evening. He said:

Yes, she should break the fast even if it is almost sunset.

2. Then the Imam was asked what a woman should do who becomes free of menstruation at the beginning of the day (after dawn), performs her ritual bath and has not yet eaten anything. He answered:

She must not fast that day. Any blood during a day of fasting voids the fast.

3. About a woman whose menstruation stops at the beginning of the day he said:

She should pray and fast for the rest of the day, then make up the entire day of fasting.

## T - Age of Obligation for Fasting

1.  When Imam al-Sadiq was asked how old a youth should be before it becomes obligatory for him to fast he answered:

    Fourteen or fifteen years of age. If he fasts before that, then let him.

2.  He also stated:

    When a youth is capable of fasting three consecutive days, then it is obligatory for him to fast the month of Ramadan.

3.  Imam al-Sadiq said:

    We instruct our boys to fast when they are seven years old for as much as they are capable, whether half a day, more than half, or less. When hunger or thirst overcomes them, they break the fast. In this way they become accustomed to fasting and are able to do it when they grow older. When your young boys reach the age of nine, instruct them to fast as much as they are capable, and when thirst overcomes them, allow them to break their fast.

4.  Imam Musa ibn Ja'far was asked when it becomes obligatory for a youth to fast and pray. He said:

    When he reaches sexual maturity and is acquainted with prayer and fasting.

## U - Voluntary Fasting

### i.  The virtues of voluntary fasting

1.  The Prophet said:

    Allah causes whoever fasts a day voluntarily to enter the Garden.

2.  He also said:

    Forgiveness is obligatory upon one who fasts, seeking Allah's recompense.

3. And:

> Whoever fasts a day in the way of Allah it is as though he fasted a year.

4. The mother of 'Ammarah offered the Messenger of Allah food when he visited her while some of the people with him were fasting. He told them:

> When food is eaten in the presence of one who is fasting the angels bless him.

### ii. The voluntary fast of the guest or host

The Messenger of Allah said:

> When a man enters a country or place other than his own, he is the guest of the people of their way of life in that place until he leaves them. It is not proper for the guest to fast but with the permission of his hosts so that they may accord him what is his due as a guest. Also, it is not proper for the host to fast except with the guest's permission, so that the guest does not feel shy about wanting food when he is hungry and does not leave his host after restraining himself.

## V - Continuous Fasting (*sawm al-dahr*)

1. Imam 'Ali said:

> Fasting the Month of Patience (Ramadan) and three days every month removes anxiety and confusion from the heart. Fasting three days every month is like the continuous fast, for whoever does a good action has his reward multiplied ten times.

2. He described the fasting of the Messenger of Allah saying:

> The Messenger of Allah used to fast continuously as Allah willed, then stopped doing that and fasted on Mondays and Thursdays; then he stopped and fasted the three days of the full moon every month, until Allah took possession of him.

3.  Imam al-Sadiq said:

    The Messenger of Allah fasted until it was said that he never
    broke his fast. Then he fasted the fast of David, fasting on
    alternate days. Then he fasted three days of the month,
    referring to it as the "continuous fast which eliminates the
    whisperings of the heart". Someone asked which days these
    were and the Messenger responded: "The first Thursday of
    the first ten days, the first Wednesday of the second ten days,
    and the last Thursday of the last ten days". A man asked:
    "How is it that these days became the days of fasting?" The
    Prophet replied: "Because the punishments of communities
    that preceded us occurred on these days." Thus the
    Messenger of Allah fasted on these days of fearful
    apprehension.

4.  Imam al-Sadiq said:

    The Messenger of Allah was asked about the fast of the two
    Thursdays and how it differed from the middle Wednesday
    of the second ten days. He responded: "On Thursday one's
    actions are presented and on Wednesday the Fire was
    created. As for fasting, its virtue is the Garden".

5.  Imam al-Rida said:

    Allah appointed voluntary fasts to complete the obligatory
    ones. Three days of fasting are appointed every month,
    because Allah says: "Whoever does a good deed will be
    rewarded with ten like it." Thus whoever fasts one day out of
    every ten it is as though he has fasted continuously.

6.  Salman al-Farsi said:

    The fast of three days each month is the continuous fast, and
    whoever can should fast more.

7.  Imam al-Sadiq said:

    Each Thursday the slave's actions are presented to Allah, so
    it is best that his actions are presented to Allah while he is
    fasting. Wednesday is the day on which the Fire was created
    and (on which) Allah destroyed former communities.
    Wednesday is a day of continuing misfortune, so it is best

that the slave repel from himself the misfortune of that day by fasting.

8. The same Imam was asked what one ought to do if there were two Thursdays within the last ten days of the month, and he replied:

Fast the first, for you may not reach the second.

9. Imam al-Sadiq was asked what one should do if one does not fast the three days of every month because it is distressing for him. He recommended that:

A portion of food (a mudd) should be given for every day.

10. A man came to the Imam and said:

It is very difficult for me to fast three days every month. Can I give charity in the amount of a Dirham for every day?

The Imam said:

The charity of a Dirham is better in your case than fasting.

11. He was also asked:

Can I delay fasting three days each month from summer to winter? I find that much easier to do.

The Imam replied:

Yes, you may do so.

12. The Prophet said:

A woman cannot fast voluntarily without her husband's permission.

13. Imam 'Ali ibn al-Husayn said:

The fasts that are prohibited are fasting on the Eid after the month of Ramadan, the Eid of the Pilgrimage and the three days following it known as "The days of Drying the Meat", and fasting on the Day of Doubt (i.e. fasting Ramadan when one doubts whether it is Ramadan or still Sha'ban). Furthermore, fasting continuously (i.e. every day) is prohibited.

## W - Recommended Fasts

### i.  *The fasts of Rajab and Sha'ban*

Among the other recommended fasts is the fast of the months of Rajab and Sha'ban (the months immediately before and after Ramadan).

1.  The Prophet said:

    > Sha'ban is my month and the best of months after Ramadan. On the Day of Reckoning I shall intercede for whoever fasts one day of Sha'ban.

2.  Imam al-Sadiq was asked whether any of his forefathers ever fasted Sha'ban. He replied:

    > The best of fathers, the Messenger of Allah, fasted it.

3.  He also said:

    > Allah records a fast of two consecutive months for whoever fasts the last three days of Sha'ban, connecting them to Ramadan. The mistakes of the one who fasts Ramadan in faith and contentment leave him so that he is like what he was the day he was born.

### ii.  *The fast of Nawruz*

Nawruz is the first day of spring and the Persian New Year. Imam al-Sadiq said:

> On the day of Nawruz, bathe, dress in your cleanest clothes, perfume yourself with scent and fast.

### iii.  *Misconceptions about fasting on the days of 'Ashura ($10^{th}$ Muharram) and 'Arafat ( $9^{th}$ Dhu'l-Hajj)*

1.  Someone said to Imam al-Sadiq:

    > They assert that fasting on the day of 'Arafat is equivalent to one year's fasting.

The Imam replied:

My father did not fast it.

The man then asked:

Why did he not fast it?

The Imam said:

The day of 'Arafat is a day of supplication, and he was afraid that if he fasted, it would distract him from supplication and prayer. Also, he did not like fasting it lest the day of 'Arafat be the day of the Eid, and fasting is not permissible on that day.

2.  Imam al-Baqir was asked about the fast of 'Ashura' and he replied:

Fasting 'Ashura' was performed before the month of Ramadan was enjoined. When Allah enjoined fasting the month of Ramadan, the fast of 'Ashura' was abandoned.

3.  When Imam al-Sadiq was asked about fasting on the day of 'Arafat he replied:

It is a major day of celebration [implying one does not fast] and invocation of Allah.

Then he was asked:

And what about the day of 'Ashura?'

He replied:

On that day Husayn (the son of 'Ali) was killed, so if you are one who enjoys the misfortune of others, then fast.

Then he added:

The Umayyad family vowed to kill Husayn and then took that day as a day of celebration, fasting it in thanks, their children rejoicing. This became a traditional practice with the family of Abu Sufyan up to this day. Certainly, fasting is not practised to mark a calamity or disaster but for wellbeing. Husayn suffered affliction on the day of 'Ashura', so if you are one who suffers affliction by what happened to him, then do not fast. If, however, you are one who gloats over misfortune, gladdened by the success of the Banu Umayyah, then fast, giving thanks to Allah.

# Chapter Five

# The Rules of Fasting According to Ja'fari Law

The path of Islam and its code of conduct encompasses every aspect of life. In order to reach correct decisions in all aspects of worship or other aspects of the life-transaction, it is not always possible or practical for every Muslim to possess the entirety of that knowledge. Thus Muslim scholars and men of erudition and piety emerged to spend a considerable time studying the Qur'an and the Prophetic way, along with other relevant fields of knowledge, in order to arrive at a level of competence to expound upon matters of Islamic ritual and law. This specialised discipline forms the backbone of jurisprudence in Islam.

This chapter and the next present the most salient rules about fasting in Islam. In this chapter we find the regulations that reflect the legal opinions of the most prominent scholars of the Ja'fari School, which follows the teachings of the Prophet as transmitted by his Household. The Shi'ite Imams or Ahl al-Bayt take their tradition from the Prophet's Household. The Imams have said: "What we tell you was narrated by my father on the strength of his father reaching back to the Prophet."

In chapter six we will explain the same rules according to the four Sunni Schools, which reach their verdicts by taking traditions from Companions. It will be noticed that any variation bewteen the Ja'fari and Sunni schools of law are as minor as those between the Sunni schools themselves.

Those unacquainted with law texts may find the detail and style of presentation somewhat turgid, as one would expect with legal information. We respectfully suggest that the reader bears in mind that the ritual practices of Islam establish a discipline as the means to an end, which is enlightenment and inner contentment. The guidelines set down by Islamic law seek to describe clearly the form of the way of life that can bring about the fruition of man's inner potential. Later on, in chapter nine, we will see how the forms reflect meaning and thus come to understand that without the form leading to meaning and transfor-mation the path becomes empty, incomplete and barren. This present chapter can serve as a useful reference whenever a legal question arises regarding the rules of fasting. Many of the points mentioned are difficult to remember, and on occasion one needs clarification on matters of doubt.

## A. Conditions for Fulfilling the Obligation to Fast

It is obligatory for every responsible person to fast the month of Ramadan. This means that one must refrain from everything which would invalidate the fast from the time of the *adhan* of the dawn prayer until the sun has set. It is necessary that this fast be accompanied by a specific intention to fast the days of the month of Ramadan (so as to attain nearness to Allah). The following conditions must be met in order to fulfill the obligation to fast:

1. Maturity.

2. Sound reason.

3. Consciousness. If one loses consciousness during the fast but regains it before sunset, the fast should be completed as a measure of precaution.

4. Purity from menstruation and post-natal bleeding.

5. Safety and security (i.e. not under threat from an enemy), that is, well-being which ensures that one would not be harmed by the fast. This includes one's person, wealth, and dignity, as well as those of others. (If fasting under such stress one's behaviour might become erratic).

6. Being in the area of one's residence or town [see the appendix on Abbreviated Prayers]. With regard to the locations wherein one may choose to either perform abbreviated or complete

prayers, like the Sacred Mosque in Makkah, it is not permissible for a traveller to fast there.

7. One who is travelling should note the following:

    a. A traveller is required to have passed the permissible boundaries as applicable to abbreviated prayers before breaking the fast.

    b. One who travels after the sun has begun to descend from its zenith must complete his fast.

    c. If a traveller returns to his domicile or residence before or after the sun has begun to descend from its zenith and he has not been refraining from that which invalidates the fast, he does not fast. If, however, he returns to his domicile or residence before the sun has begun to descend from its zenith and he has not done anything which would invalidate the fast, he must make the intention to fast and complete the fast.

    d. If a traveller fasts due to ignorance of the regulation, and then finds out about the regulation after sunset, his fast is considered to be correct and valid.

    e. It is permissible to travel unnecessarily during Ramadan, although it is most prudent (*ahwat*) to travel only when it is necessary.

    f. It is reprehensible (*makruh*) for the non-fasting traveller and any others who are permitted not to fast to engage in a lot of eating, drinking, and sexual intercourse during the day.

8. Those who are exempt from fasting:

    a. The Elderly

    The elderly who are too weak to fast and those who suffer from polydipsia* are exempt from the obligation

---

* An illness which renders one incapable of quenching one's thirst.

to fast if they find that fasting is too difficult for them; however, they should only eat and drink what is necessary to maintain their well-being. They are also required to offer a compensation for each day they miss (one kilogram of either wheat, flour, bread, or rice). It is also prudent to give twice that amount.

b.  The Pregnant

A pregnant woman who is close to the time of giving birth is exempt from fasting if she fears for the well-being of her child. In this instance she is required to compensate for each day missed by giving one kilogram of the above-mentioned foodstuffs. If, however, she fears for her own well-being rather than that of her child, she is not required to give compensation for missed days.

c.  Nursing women

A nursing woman who does not have adequate milk is exempt from fasting if she fears that fasting will bring harm to her child. She may break her fast and pay an indemnity (*kaffarah*) of one kilo of food per day. If, however, she fears that she herself will be harmfully affected by fasting, she need only make up the fasts later and no compensation is required of her.

d.  The Sick

The regulation concerning the sick is that if one recovers from an illness before the sun's descent from its zenith, he should refrain from any further eating if he has already eaten something, and he must make up that day later on. If he has not eaten anything, then he must formulate the intention to fast and continue to fast that day. If, however, one recovers after the descent of the sun from its zenith, then he need not fast, nor is it necessary for him to abstain from eating for the remainder of the day.

## B. The Intention (*Niyyah*) to Fast

1. It is obligatory to make the intention to refrain from everything which invalidates the fast from the beginning of dawn until the legal time of sunset out of the desire for proximity to Allah.

2. It is obligatory that one specify in his intention the type of fast he intends to perform. For example, a compensatory fast, a vicarious fast being carried out on someone else's behalf, or a fast undertaken as an indemnity (*kaffarah*) for some action or omission.

3. Intending to refrain from all things that invalidate the fast is sufficient as an intention and there is no need for specific details.

4. When one omits to make the necessary intention during the month of Ramadan, there are a number of circumstances to be considered:

   a. If one remember before the sun has started to descend from its zenith, he must refrain from eating and it is most prudent (*ahwat*) that he make up that day later.

   b. If one remember after the sun has started to descend, his fast on that day is valid.

   c. It is permissible to make the intention to fast a supererogatory (*mustahabb*) fast, even if this be done just before the sun sets, provided one has refrained from all that breaks the fast for the entire day.

5. It is necessary that one's intention to fast be maintained for the duration of the fasting day as continuity of intention is mandatory. One intention at the beginning of the month of Ramadan suffices provided that it is maintained for the entire duration of the month.

6. If one makes an intention in the evening to fast the next day, and then goes to sleep and does not awaken the entire day, the fast is considered to be valid.

## C. Supererogatory, Reprehensible and Forbidden Fasts

1. It is not permissible for one who is required to make up missed days of obligatory fasting to fast supererogatory fasts until he has made up the obligatory ones.

2. It is reprehensible (*makruh*) to fast on the day of 'Ashura', the tenth of Muharram (The first month of the Islamic calendar).

3. It is forbidden (*haram*) to fast on the two days of Eid.

4. It is forbidden (*haram*) to fast with the intention of fasting Ramadan on a day in which there is doubt as to whether it is the last day of Sha'ban or the first of Ramadan. It is, however, permissible to fast that day without specifying it as a fast of Ramadan, until and unless it be confirmed as such later.

## D. Actions which Invalidate the Fast

Actions which invalidate the fast are of two kinds: firstly, those that require a compensatory fast (*qada*) as well as an expiatory fast (*kaffarah*), and secondly, those that only require a compensatory fast.

1. The following actions are of the first kind, that is, they require the fast to be compensated for as well as expiated:

    a. Intentionally eating or drinking: Both invalidate the fast. It makes no difference whether the food or drink is of the normal kind or otherwise, or whether it is of a small or large amount. This rule applies even were food or drink to enter the body by way of an opening other than the mouth, e.g. the nose. Furthermore, intentionally swallowing remaining food particles lodged between the teeth also invalidates the fast. Eating or drinking unintentionally or due to forgetfulness does not break the fast.

    b. Sexual intercourse: All types of sexual intercourse invalidate the fast. It does not matter whether the sexual intercourse is heterosexual or homosexual (which is in itself forbidden), with a human or an animal (which is also in itself forbidden). This rule applies even if one were unaware that sexual intercourse during the fast is forbidden. If, however, sexual intercourse is unintentional, such as in the case of rape or other circumstances wherein one is forced to take part in intercourse, the fast will not be invalidated. From the standpoint of Islamic law, sexual intercourse is considered to have taken place once the head of the penis penetrates the opening. In the event of sexual intercourse during the fast, this regulation applies to both parties except where compulsion has taken place.

c. Intentional ejaculation of semen by way of masturbation, sensual touch, or any other means: The fast is not invalidated by unintentional ejaculation unless one indulge in touching or looking at one's own or another's private parts when one knows that such activity usually stimulates ejaculation. Likewise, involuntary emission of semen during daylight sleeping does not invalidate the fast.

d. Intentionally remaining in the state of *janabah* (i.e. following intercourse) until the time of the dawn (*subh*) prayer: This rule specifically applies to the fasts of the month of Ramadan and its compensatory fasts. It is, however, better to apply this regulation to all types of obligatory fasts. Not performing the proper ritual bath (*ghusl*) upon completing a menstruation or a period of post-natal bleeding is equivalent to remaining in the state of *janabah* (only insofar as the month of Ramadan is concerned).

A person who enters the state of *janabah* during the night and then awakens after the dawn prayer is governed by the same regulation that governs one who intentionally remains in that state (until dawn) unless he intended to take a ritual bath before dawn. If he intended to perform a ritual bath before dawn, or it were his habit to rise before dawn, then his fast will be valid unless he went back to sleep again after awakening without having first taken a ritual bath.

The fast of a person who knows he is in the state of *janabah* and forgets to take a ritual bath until dawn will be invalid and he must make up the fast. It is permissible to perform a dry ablution with earth (*tayammum*) in lieu of a ritual bath when it is impossible to take one during the night before dawn.

e.  Intentionally immersing oneself in water. There is no difference between this and submersing only one's head in water.

f.  Intentionally lying about Allah, His Prophet, the Imams of the household of the Prophet, and, as a precaution, all of the prophets and messengers.

g.  Intentionally causing thick dust, and as a precaution fine dust (which includes smoke), to enter the throat.

h.  Intentionally vomiting. If, however, something comes up as a result of an involuntary belch, this does not negate the fast. Likewise, if one vomit unintentionally due to sickness, his fast remains valid.

i.  Taking an enema with any fluid even if it is because of an illness. It is permissible to use something other that liquid in an enema unless it will in effect give nourishment.

The above listed actions, if undertaken during the fast, necessitate the invalidated fast both to made up and expiated. Both of these obligations are detailed as follows:

2.  Regulation Governing Expiation or Indemnity (*kaffarah*)

a.  The Combined or Major Expiation: This is required of one who intentionally invalidates his fast during the month of Ramadan with something which is in itself forbidden (*haram*), such as attributing a lie to Allah or His Prophet, drinking alcoholic beverages, committing fornication, etc. In these instances, one must pay a Major Expiation which is the combination of three expiatory acts as follows:

i.   Feeding sixty needy people.

ii.  Manumission (freeing) a slave.

iii. Fasting two consecutive months. This may be accomplished by fasting one complete lunar month and one day or more of the following month and then completing the remainder of the second month at another time.

b.  The Single or Minor Expiation: This is required of one who intentionally invalidates the fast during the month of Ramadan with an action that is not forbidden (*haram*) in itself. In this instance one must execute one of the three expiatory acts mentioned above, that is, either freeing a slave, or fasting two consecutive months, or feeding sixty needy people.

c.  Expiation and penalty: If a man compel his wife to have sexual intercourse during the fast of the month of Ramadan, it is considered more prudent (*ahwat*) that he be required to pay two expiations and undergo two penalties of twenty-five lashes each, a total of fifty lashes, thereby assuming the legal responsibilities of both himself and his wife. This applies equally to couples of both permanent and temporary marriages. If, however, a woman compels her husband to have sexual intercourse, she is not obliged to assume the legal responsibilities of her husband.

An expiation must be repeated if the action is repeated on a daily basis, that is, one expiation for each day in which one has committed one or more actions which invalidate the fast. Intercourse and masturbation are governed by a different regulation in that one must pay an expiation for each time that they are done, even if they be committed a number of times during the space of one day.

If a man be not fasting due to a valid excuse and he compel his fasting wife to have sexual intercourse with him, he is not required to pay her indemnity, nor is she required to pay his.

There are a number of points which must be noted here:

i.  One who breaks his fast intentionally and then travels is not relieved of his responsibility to pay the indemnity required of him.

ii.  One who intentionally invalidates his fast during the month of Ramadan must continue to abstain from all that invalidates the fast for the remainder of the day and pay the relevant indemnity.

iii.  Indemnity is required of those who have knowledge of the regulations governing this matter. They are not obligatory for those who are unaware.

iv.  Whoever is compelled or forced to break the fast during the month of Ramadan should restrict himself to that which is absolutely necessary. He is then obliged to perform a compensatory fast, but he does not have to pay any indemnity. This rule also applies to one who breaks his fast invoking *taqiyyah.*

3.  Fast-invalidating actions which only require the fast to be made up. There are a number of actions which invalidate the fast and only require a compensatory fast, but no indemnity:

---

* Hiding one's religion in dire circumstances such as persecution or threat to one's life.

a.  Whoever breaks a fast in the month of Ramadan for an acceptable reason, such as travel, sickness, etc. must perform a compensatory fast at another time of the year, but not on the days in which fasting is forbidden. This rule applies equally to those who have been compelled or forced to break their fast.

b.  Whoever does not cease to eat at dawn or breaks his fast before sunset thinking that the sun has set, without first inquiring or making sure, must make up the fast for that day. A compensatory fast is not required if the person had made an inquiry, or was certain, and then discovered that he had been mistaken.

c.  If one neglects to make the necessary intention to perform a fast in the month of Ramadan but does not commit any of the aforementioned actions which invalidate the fast, he must only perform a compensatory prayer.

d.  If one commits any of the actions which invalidate the fast without investigating whether he committed the fast-invalidating act, he need only perform a compensatory fast. If, however, he had investigated and was certain that it was still night-time, but subsequently discovered that it had really been dawn when he committed the act, he is not required to perform a compensatory fast for that day and his fast is considered valid.

e.  If one does not abstain from that which invalidates the fast, relying upon information that is still night-time, but then discovers that dawn had indeed arrived, he must perform a compensatory fast for that day.

f.  Emergency fast-breaking: If someone fasting becomes thirsty to such an extent that he feels he will either lose consciousness or bring about the deterioration of his health because of dehydration, he is permitted to eat or drink whatever amount is necessary to retain his well-being. This rule also applies to one who is unable to bear the weakness caused by the lack of food. In both these cases the person in question must only eat or drink what is necessary and then resume fasting. He may, however, take nourishment again as many times as necessary before sunset provided such nourishment is an absolute necessity. (This rule is of particular benefit to those living in areas where the daytime is unusually long, like in northern countries where day light may last for twenty hours or more in midsummer.) A person experiencing these types of difficulties with fasting is required compensate for each day missed.

g. Regulations governing the delay in making up missed fasts:

i. The time for a compensatory fast for a missed fast of the month of Ramadan extends throughout the year. It is possible for a person to make up the fast whenever he or she wishes. It is, however, considered more prudent not to delay it until the next Ramadan. Should it be delayed beyond that date, it remains a standing obligation.

ii. If one deliberately delay making up a missed fast from Ramadan until the next Ramadan, he must expiate each delayed fast with approximately one kilo of food, as well as making them up. If he be obliged to make up a fast as a result of having intentionally broken a fast during Ramadan, he must pay two indemnities: one for intentionally breaking the fast, which is either freeing a slave, feeding sixty poor people, or fasting two consecutive months (or a combination of all three if the fast were intentionally broken with a forbidden action) together with an indemnity for delaying the compensatory fast, which is approximately one kilo of food.

iii. If the exemption allowing one to abstain from fasting during Ramadan continues until the next Ramadan, the performance of a compensatory fast is no longer necessary, but one must still compensate for each missed day of fasting with approximately two pounds of food.

iv. It is permissible to give the indemnity of numerous missed fasts of one or more Ramadans to one poor person.

## E. Confirming the New Moon of the Month of Ramadan

1. The obligation to fast the month of Ramadan comes into effect once the sighting of the new moon has been confirmed in one of the following ways:

   a. The legally responsible person *(mukallaf)* sees the new moon himself.

   b. He is certain or assured of its sighting by the community.

   c. 30 days of the month of Sha'ban (8th month of the Islamic lunar calendar) have passed.

   d. Two upright men (defined as those who refrain from that which is forbidden and execute their religious obligations) bear witness to having sighted the new moon marking the beginning of the lunar month of Ramadan.

   e. The judgement of the *mujtahid* who is considered to be the legitimate legal authority *(al-hakimu ash-shar'i)* that it is the first of the month of Ramadan (even if one is not an emulator of that particular *mujtahid*).

2. Regulations governing the Sighting of the New Moon

   a. If one has not begun to fast and then discovers that the moon had been sighted, he must refrain from all that invalidates the fast for the remainder of the day and then make up the fast for that day at a later time.

b. It is sufficient that the new moon be sighted in another land, area, or country.

c. It is not permissible to cease fasting the daily fast of the month of Ramadan until the new moon of the month of Shawwal (the month which immediately follows Ramadan) has been sighted. Once the new moon of the month of Shawwal has been sighted, fasting must cease.

## F. Recommended (*mustahabb*) Fasts

It is recommended that one fast the following days:

1. The first and last Thursday of every month and the first Wednesday after the tenth of the month. This fast is called the Fast of the Epoch (*sawm al-dahr*).

2. The thirteenth, fourteenth, and fifteenth of every month.

3. Some or all of the months of Rajab and Sha'ban.

4. The 25th and 29th of Dhu'l Qa'dah (the 25th being the day the earth was spread out).

5. The day of the festival of Nawruz (the spring equinox, the 21st of March).

6. The first through to the ninth of Dhu'l-Hijjah.

7. The 18th of Dhu'l-Hijjah (the anniversary of the event of Ghadir Khum).

8. The first and the third of Muharram.

9. The birthday of the Prophet, the 17th of Rabi'u 'l-Awwal.

10. The anniversary of the beginning of the prophetic mission of Muhammad, the 27th of Rajab.

## G. Recommended (*mustahabb*) Actions for those Fasting

1. Occupying oneself with remembrance of Allah (*dhikr*), seeking forgiveness, glorifying Allah, supplication, and sending prayers upon the Prophet Muhammad and his family, upon all of them be peace.

2. Reciting the Holy Qur'an.

3. Offering food to those fasting in order that they may break their fast at the end of the day.

4. Generosity towards one's brothers and sisters and maintaining contact with one's relatives.

5. Visiting the sick and participating in funeral processions.

6. Partaking of the pre-dawn meal (*suhur*), even if it is only a drink of water.

7. It is related from Imam Baqir that he said: 'If you fast then let your ears, eyes, hair, and skin fast.' He also said: 'Do not let your day of fasting be like a day when you are not fasting.'

## H. Actions which are Permissible for those Fasting

There are certain actions which one may undertake without invalidating the fast. They are as follows:

1. Medicinal injections into the veins, muscles, tissue etc.

2. Using eye-drops, nose-drops or ear drops.

3. Brushing one's teeth provided whatever remains in the mouth in terms of water, toothpaste, etc. is expelled.

4. Tasting food and chewing it for an infant provided that all the food is removed from the mouth afterwards.

5. Rinsing the mouth (*madmadah*) at the time of ablution (*wudu'*). If water is consumed unintentionally during such rinsing, the following regulations must be observed:

    a.  If the consumption occurs while rinsing the mouth prior to an ablution which is being performed for an obligatory prayer (*salat*), one's fast remains valid.

    b.  If it occurs while rinsing the mouth prior to an ablution which is being performed for a non-obligatory prayer, the fast must be made up.

    c.  If it occurs while rinsing the mouth for a reason other than ablution, the fast must be made up.

## I.  Actions that are Reprehensible (*makruh*) for those Fasting

1. Smelling aromatic plants, especially the narcissus flower.

2. Wetting the garments on the body.

3. Engaging in activity that might cause sexual arousal.

4. Using antimony (kohl), musk, or aloe on the eyes.

5. Composing [frivolous] poetry.

6. Cupping or drawing blood or other such actions which bring about weakness.

7. Putting drops of oil in the ears.

8. Bathing if it will cause one to become weak.

9. Speech which is not beneficial.

10. Generally everything which distracts the limbs, mind and heart from worship and seeking nearness to Allah.

## J.  *I'tikaf* (Retreat, Temporary Residence in a Mosque)

*I'tikaf* is to take up temporary residence in a Mosque with the intention of devoting oneself to the worship of Allah. The most meritorious time for *i'tikaf* is during the last ten days of Ramadan.

In addition to soundness of mind and faith (*iman*), the following conditions are also necessary for *i'tikaf*:

1. One must make the intention of seeking closeness to Allah.

2. One must be fasting (so *i'tikaf* is not possible while travelling).

3. The minimum number of days for *i'tikaf* is three. Any additional days are valid.

4. *I'tikaf* must take place in one of four mosques, which are: the Sacred Mosque (*al-Masjid al-Haram*) in Makkah, the Mosque of the Prophet in Madinah, the Mosque of Kufah, the Mosque of Basrah, or in the main mosque of one's locale. The term mosque here also includes its roof, basement, and ancillary buildings.

5. A person must obtain the permission of one whose permission is necessary in order for the *i'tikaf* to be permissible, for example, a wife needs the permission of her husband and a child needs the permission of his or her father.

6. A person in *i'tikaf* must remain within the mosque and not leave it unless it becomes absolutely necessary to do so, for example, if he needs to take a ritual bath, go to the toilet, or attend to an obligation or supererogation prescribed by Islamic law, such as attending a funeral or visiting the sick. It is prudent not to sit or stay outside the mosque, nor change the form or manner of the *i'tikaf*.

7. One performing *i'tikaf* must refrain from:

   a. Sexual contact, even enjoying the company of one's wife, and likewise masturbation (something forbidden in any case).

   b. Smelling flowers or aromatic flowers or plants.

   c. Dealing in trade and worldly pursuits (this will not invalidate the trading, but rather the *i'tikaf*).

   d. Arguing over worldly matters.

## K. Alms Given at the Conclusion of Ramadan

The alms given at the end of Ramadan (*zakat al-fitr*) have been called the 'alms of the individual', because it is levied on individuals and not on property. The alms become obligatory upon a person on the eve of the Eid festival which marks the end of Ramadan.

1. The following requirements are necessary:

   a. Maturity.

   b. Soundness of mind, that is, one must not suffer from any mental disorder and not be in a state of unconsciouness on the eve of the Eid.

   c. Having the unrestricted right to dispose of one's own property without legal impediment.

   d. Financial independence, that is, one has sufficient provisions for the year or has the potential or possibility of obtaining what is considered sufficient.

2. The time of payment is the beginning of the night, beginning at sunset until the sun begins to descend from its zenith on the day of Eid.

   a. If one sets aside the alms required of him at that time, he may pay it after the stated time.

   b. It is not permissible for one to pay alms before its time unless it has been given as a loan. The loan is then nullified when the time for payment of alms comes (i.e. it becomes considered the *fitra*).

   c. It is advisable not to pay the alms in another locale.

3. It is obligatory for those who meet the above mentioned requirements to give these alms on their own behalf and on behalf of living members of their families.

   a. This does not include a guest, who is not considered part of the family, or an employee like a servant or a gardener, if they bear the responsibility for their own livelihood.

b.  It is recommended that an individual who is poor give the alms to a member of his own family.

4.  What may be given:

a.  Wheat, barley, dates, or raisins.

b.  It is permissible to give the amount in cash.

c.  It is preferable that the alms be paid in whatever form is most useful.

d.  The amount is calculated according to the time of the taxation in the particular locale, the amount being approximately three kilograms of any of the above mentioned foods or their monetary equivalent.

5.  Like the tax levied on property it is considered prudent to spend it on the poor.

a.  In the absence of people of true faith, it is permissible to donate the alms to the poor and the deprived even if they are not fully committed to the practices of Islam.

b.  Those who drink alcohol, who have stopped praying or who would spend it in disobedience should not be given alms.

c.  Muslims who trace their lineage to the Prophet's family can only accept alms from other Muslims who also trace their lineage to the Prophet.

## L.  The Eid Prayer

The proper time for the Eid prayer is from the time the sun rises above the horizon until it reaches its zenith. According to the Ja'fari school these prayers are only considered obligatory when the Imam Mahdi, the final Saviour of Islam, is present; until then, however, they are recommended. The regulations governing these prayers are as follows:

1. The Eid prayer for either festival is performed in the same manner. It consists of two cycles, in which the opening chapter of the Qur'an and another complete chapter are recited while standing. It is best to recite Surah al-A'la in the first cycle and Surat al-Shams in the second, or Surat al-Shams in the first and Surah al-Ghashiyah in the second.

2. After the recitation of the Qur'an in the first cycle, one should perform five magnifications (*Takbir*: *'Allahu Akbar'*), each one followed by a supplication recited with the palms of one's hands extended upward.

3. The second cycle has four magnifications, each followed by a supplication in the same accompanying posture.

4. Any prayer or words in remembrance of Allah are permissible during the supplications. Certain ones are recommended and can be found in several available manuals.

5. A preliminary bath of purification is considered to be a practice which the Prophet followed on the days of the two Eids.

6. Performing the customary call to prayer before the Eid prayer is not recommended. Instead the *Mu'adhdhan* (the person calling people to prayer) should say *'As-salah'* (literally: 'the prayer') three times.

7. The Eid prayer should preferably be performed outdoors.

8. The prayer-leader should come out barefooted and quietly. It is preferable that he use perfume and wear his cleanest clothing.

9. If the prayer-leader has doubts about whether he performed any part of the prayer, he should perform it, but if he has already passed the part which he has doubts about, he should proceed with the prayer.

10. The homily given by the prayer-leader is given after the prayer.

# Chapter Six

# The Rules of Fasting According to Sunni Schools of Law

The Sunni movement and theology diversified and developed into four schools of law approximately 200 years after the Prophet. Each school follows the rulings of a different, prominent Sunni scholar, all living within a hundred years of each other. Abu Hanifah, Malik ibn Anas, Muhammad ibn Idris al-Shafi'i, and Ahmed ibn Hanbal were all legislators of Muslim Law in their time whose rulings were amplified, particularly in response to the political need for codifying Islamic law. This chapter provides a comparative treatise of fasting according to these four schools.

Like the followers of the Ahl al-Bayt, the four schools of law have classed fasting four ways: obligatory, recommended, forbidden, and reprehensible. The same fasts are obligatory for them as they are for the Ja'faris, except for fasting during the Pilgrimage and retreat (i'tikaf).

## A - Conditions of the Obligation

As has already been observed, the fast of Ramadan is an obligation binding upon all responsible (mukallaf) Muslims. A responsible Muslim is one who has reached puberty and is of sound mind. The fast is not an obligation for the madman when he is in a state of madness, nor would his fast be considered acceptable if he were to fast. Young children are not obliged to fast, but were a child to fast, the fast would be considered correct if he or she were at a stage where they can discriminate. The fast is not accepted from those who are outside the fold of Islam. The four schools all agree that one who refrains from eating without proper intention does not perform an acceptable fast.

## B – Conditions that break the Fast

1. All four schools agree that fasting cannot take place during menstruation and post-natal bleeding which may recur for forty days after childbirth.

2. Regarding sickness, there are differences between the schools. All four say that if a fasting person becomes ill and fears that fasting may aggravate his condition or delay his cure, he may break his fast if he so wish, but it is not necessary for him to do so. On the other hand, should he suspect that he may die or lose any of his faculties he must stop immediately.

3. All four schools agree that one who suffers from chronic, health-threatening thirst is not required to fast. If he or she can make it up later they must do so without paying any indemnity (*kaffarah*). There is a difference of opinion regarding malnutrition, as to whether it brings about a condition which warrants breaking the fast like severe thirst. The four schools hold that they are the same: all permit one to break the fast.

4. All four schools hold that should the nursing mother or pregnant woman be afraid for herself or her child, her fast is improper and she is allowed to break it. If she does so, she must make it up subsequently. All agree upon this but differ on the form of compensation.

   According to the Hanafis a compensation is not required; the Malikis contend that the nursing mother must provide a compensation but not the pregnant woman. The Hanbalis and Shafi'is say that compensation is required from pregnant women or nursing mothers alike only if they are afraid for the child. If either woman be afraid for herself as well she must make up the fast but without paying an indemnity. The compensation for each day that she has broken is one '*mudd*', which is the quantity of grain that would feed one poor person, equivalent in the present day to approximately 750 grams of wheat of similar foodstuff.

5. Truncating the prayers because of travel is a condition that obliges only the Hanafis to break their fast, because they consider shortening the prayers obligatory. The other schools allow the option of shortening prayers while travelling or to pray the full prayers. The conditions for abbreviating prayers are included further on.

6. The aged are permitted to break the fast if they find difficulty in fasting. For each day missed they must feed someone in need by way of indemnity. The same applies to the sick person who has no hope of recovering before the next Ramadan. All schools agree that the indemnity is obligatory, except for the Hanbalis, who say it is only recommended.

## C - Removal of the Cause for Breaking the Fast

The Shafi'is hold that whenever the cause which permitted the fast to be broken is removed, as in the case of an ill person recovering, a boy reaching maturity, a traveller arriving home or a menstruating woman becoming purified, it is recommended that one practise abstinence for the remainder of the day as a courtesy and exercise of discipline. The Hanafis and Hanbalis both contend that abstention is obligatory. The Malikis hold that it is neither necessary nor recommended.

## D – Unconsciousness and Intoxication

Shafi'is hold that the fast of someone who is intoxicated or unconscious is not valid if he be out of his senses for the entire period of the fast. If, however, he be out of his senses for only part of the fast, then his fast is valid for the rest of the day but he must make up the day as well. The fast must be made up whether he was unconscious as a result of his own doing or not. Making up the fast is not binding on the intoxicated person unless his intoxication were by his own doing.

Malikis contend that neither the fast of the one who is intoxicated or unconscious is correct (*maqbul*) if he were in either state for all or some of the time from dawn to sunset. If, however, this state should last for half the day or less and he were conscious at the time of formulating the intention to fast, then he does not have to make up the fast. For Malikis the time to formulate the intention to fast is from the sunset of the night before up until dawn.

The Hanafis hold that one who has become unconscious is like one who is mad. If the madness or state of unconsciousness endures for the entire month of Ramadan, then one does not have to make up the fast. If it lasts for only part of the month, then one fasts upon coming to one's senses and makes up what was missed.

Hanbalis hold that one who is intoxicated or unconscious must make up the fast whether it were on account of his own actions or not.

## E – Intentionally Breaking the Fast

1. Eating or drinking intentionally will nullify the fast. The four schools agree that the fast must be made up, but only the Hanafis say that it is obligatory to perform an expiation. The Shafi'is and Hanbalis hold that this is not obligatory.

   Whoever forgets that he is fasting and inadvertently breaks it does not have to make up his fast nor expiate his fault. This is the ruling of all schools except the Malikis, who say that it is required of him to make up the day. Smoking intentionally is included with eating and drinking.

2. Intentionally engaging in sexual intercourse is considered by all schools to nullify the fast. One must make it up and expiate

the omission. The expiation is the manumission of a slave. If a slave cannot be found, then one must fast for two consecutive months. If that cannot be done, then one must feed 60 poor people. This is the same for the Shafi'is, Hanbalis and Hanafis. For the Malikis one may choose which of the three types of expiations to perform.

As for intercourse which happens inadvertently, it does not break the fast according the the Hanafis or Shafi'is, but it does for the Hanbalis and Malikis.

3. Ejaculation will nullify the fast if it happens by choice; all schools concur on this point. If ejaculation occurs as a result of having continuously looked at something that should not be looked at during the fast, it will also render the fast void. All four schools say that the fast must be made up without any expiation due.

4. Intentional vomiting nullifies the fast. According to the Shafi'is and Malikis the fast must be made up. According to the Hanafis, if someone intentionally vomits his fast is not broken unless he vomits a full mouthful. The Hanbalis accept both these positions. All agree that if one is forced to vomit the fast is not void.

5. Cupping and bleeding according to the Hanbalis break the fast. They say that both the one who is performing it and the one upon whom it is being performed break their fasts.

6. Taking a liquid enema breaks the fast. According to all the schools the fast must be made up.

7. Using antimony around the eyes will break the fast according to the Malikis if the antimony is used in the daytime and the taste of antimony is present in the mouth.

8. If one who is meant to fast makes the intention to break his fast then refrains from doing so, as far as the Hanbalis are

concerned his fast is counted as broken. The other schools, however, do not agree with this.

## F – Actions which Necessitate Making up the Fast of Ramadan.

These cover the following areas:

1.  All four schools agree that it is necessary to make up for any days of Ramadan that have been missed within the same year; in other words, within the time between the end of the month of Ramadan and the beginning of the next Ramadan. One may choose which days to fast in order to make up the missed days except the days on which fasting is forbidden (for which see below).

2.  Whoever could have made up the missed days of Ramadan during the year but did not out of sloth must fast the next Ramadan and make up for what he had missed of the former. Additionally, all schools except the Hanbalis say that one must expiate the missed fasts by feeding one person 750 grams of wheat or grain for each day missed. The Hanafis hold that expiation is not necessary.

3.  The four schools all hold that if one who has not been able to make up the missed days between the two Ramadans because of illness is not required to make them up nor is he required to expiate them.

4.  If one had the ability to make up the fast during the year but delayed doing so with the intention of linking the days to be made up with the next Ramadan, and then something legitimate happened which prevented him or her doing so and the new month of Ramadan came upon him, he would need to make up the days only after the new month of Ramadan has been fasted without there being any expiation due from him. On this all schools agree.

5. Hanafis, Shafi'is and Hanbalis hold that the elder son of a deceased father who had broken the fast of Ramadan for a good reason and could have made up for it but did not should give 750 grams of wheat or grain as alms for every day missed. The Malikis contend that the man who is in charge of the affairs of the deceased person must pay alms for the missed days if this were stated in his will; if it were not stated in his will, the one responsible for the deceased's affairs is not required to do it.

6. All four schools hold that one who is making up a fast of Ramadan may break his fast before midday or thereafter (i.e. with good reason) without its counting against him.

## G – The Fast of Expiation

1. Shafi'is, Malikis and Hanafis hold that one who must fast two consecutive months as an expiation for having broken his fast during Ramadan is not allowed to break his fast for one day during these two months because the continuity would be broken. If he break his fast with or without reason, he must begin the whole expiation over again. Hanbalis contend that breaking the fast of these two months for a legitimate reason will not interrupt its continuity.

2. Shafi'is, Malikis and Hanafis hold that if one cannot perform any of the expiations there remains a debt upon him until he is able to do so. Hanbalis hold that if one cannot perform any of them, one is absolved of the expiation even though one may be able to do it later.

3. All agree that an expiation must be repeated again if the cause for it recurs the next day or afterwards; therefore whoever eats or drinks on two different days intentionally must perform two expiations.

4. As for one who eats, drinks and has intercourse several times in the same day, the Hanafi, Maliki and Shafi'i schools hold

that he does not have to perform more than one expiation, no matter how many times he may have committed these acts. The Hanbali school holds that if that which entailed the expiation be repeated the same day and the expiation for the first transgression had been paid before it was repeated, one must then perform another expiation. If, however, the expiation for the first transgression had not been paid before the repetition, then only one expiation need be carried out.

## H – When Fasting is Not Permissible

1.  The Maliki, Shafi'i and Hanbali schools all agree that fasting is forbidden on the Eid day following the month of Ramadan and the festival days after the day of Arafat during the Pilgrimage. The Hanafi school says that fasting on the two festivals is not forbidden but is in the highest degree undesirable.

2.  Shafi'is hold that fasting on the three days following the festival of the pilgrimage (the 11th, 12th and 13th of the month of Dhu'l-Hijjah) is not permissible. Hanbalis say that it is forbidden to fast on those days when one is not actually on the Pilgrimage, but it is not forbidden if one be on the Pilgrimage. The Hanafi school holds that fasting these days is highly desirable while the Malikis contend that fasting on the 11th and 12th of Dhu'l-Hijjah is forbidden, but not if one be on the Pilgrimage.

3.  All schools except the Hanafis agree that a woman is not permitted to perform a voluntary fast without the permission of her husband if the fast takes away one of his rights. The Hanafis, however, say that the fast of a woman performed without the permission of her husband may be undesirable but it is not forbidden.

## I - The Day of Doubt

All schools agree that when one does not fast the Day of Doubt (the day which one does not know whether it is the last day of

Sha'ban or the first day of Ramadan) and then it becomes clear that it is Ramadan, one must abstain from eating for the rest of the day and make it up later. The Shafi'is, Malikis and Hanbalis say that if one fasts the Day of Doubt and then discovers that it is actually the first of Ramadan, one is not rewarded for the fast and is not expected to make it up.

## J – Recommended Fasts

Fasting is recommended on all days of the year except for the days when fasting is forbidden. Fasting is particularly recommended on the following days by all four schools:

1.  The first Thursday of the first ten days, the first Wednesday of the second ten days, and the last Thursday of the last ten days.

2.  The 13th, 14th and 15th of each month (the days of the full moon).

3.  The day of 'Arafat, the 9th of Dhu'l-Hijjah.

4.  The months of Rajab and Sha'ban.

5.  Every Monday and Thursday.

## K – Undesirable Days for Fasting

Except for the Shafi'is, the schools specify that fasting is undesirable on Friday and Saturday, the day of Nawruz (the spring equinox).

## L – Sighting the New Moon

All four schools have agreed that whoever individually sights the crescent must act upon his knowledge, whether he sights the decrescent moon of Ramadan or the crescent one of Shawwal. Whoever has seen the crescent marking the beginning of the month of Ramadan must fast, even though not everyone else may be fasting. The Hanafis, however, say that in the case of Shawwal if one who sights the moon come before a judge and his testimony be rejected he must make up for the day he did not fast, without having to offer an expiation.

Whoever sees the crescent of Shawwal must break his fast, even though everyone else may be fasting. It makes no difference whether the one who has sighted the new moon be a just man or not, or whether they be male or female.

The schools differ on the following points, however:

1. The Hanafi, Maliki, and Hanbali schools hold that if the sighting of the crescent has been confirmed somewhere in the world, everyone else in other countries, whether near or far, must follow. The Shafi'i school holds that if the crescent has been seen in one country but not in another, then, if they are relatively close to each other, as far as the emergence of the crescent is concerned, the sighting should be followed by both countries. If they be far from each other (as far as the emergence of the crescent is concerned) each should follow its own judgement.

2. The Shafi'is, Malikis and Hanafis say that if the crescent is seen before or after midday on the 30th of Sha'ban, the day is considered the end of Sha'ban and the fast begins the following day. If the crescent be seen during the day on the 30th of Ramadan, it is considered part of Ramadan and the fast is broken the following day.

   Because the Shafi'i, Maliki and Hanafi schools contend that the crescent belongs to the last month (i.e. Sha'ban) and not to the month to come, one must therefore fast the day after the sighting if it be the end of Sha'ban, or break his fast on the day following the sighting, if it is at the end of Ramadan.

3. All schools concur that the crescent is confirmed by sight, following the Prophet's tradition which said: 'Fast upon sighting the new moon and break your fast upon its sighting'.

98

The Hanafis distinguish between the criteria for sighting the crescent of the month of Ramadan and the crescent of Shawwal. For them the crescent of Ramadan must be confirmed by one man or one woman provided they be of sound intellect and good character while the crescent of Shawwal has to be confirmed by the sight of two men or one man and two women. These conditions are only acceptable if there be a cloud cover or anything else that obstructs the horizon. Should the sky be clear, a large group of people must confirm that they have seen the crescent of Ramadan or the crescent of Shawwal.

The Shafi'is say it makes no difference whether the sky be cloudy or not. The crescent of Ramadan or Shawwal is confirmed by the witnessing of one man of reputable character provided he is Muslim and of sound intellect. The Malikis also say that the crescent of Ramadan or Shawwal has to be confirmed by two witnesses or reputable character. The Hanbalis say that the crescent of Ramadan may be confirmed by one Muslim of good character, whether male or female. As for Shawwal, it has to be confirmed by two men of good character.

4.  If no one can confirm that the crescent moon of Ramadan has been sighted, Sha'ban is considered to have been completed after 30 days. Ramadan is then begun on the following day. The Hanafis disagree with this, saying that Sha'ban is complete after 29 days. For them the following day is the first of Ramadan.

As for the crescent of Shawwal, Hanafis and Malikis contend that if the sky be cloudy after 29 days have been completed and the crescent cannot be sighted, another day is fasted and on the following day the fast must be broken. If, however, the sky be clear on the night after 30 days and the crescent is still not seen, one must fast the following day also. The witnessing of those who confirmed the beginning of the month of Ramadan would therefore be inaccurate.

Shafi'is say that breaking the fast is obligatory after the 30th day, even if the crescent of the month of Ramadan has been sighted by only one man.

Hanbalis say that if the month of Ramadan was confirmed by the sighting of the crescent by two men of reputable character it is obligatory to break the fast after the 30th. If it were confirmed by one person only, fasting is obligatory through the 31st day.

## M – Travelling and the Prayer

The four schools agree that any condition of travelling that allows the shortening of the prayers also permits breaking the fast. As observed before, Hanafis say that shortening the prayer and breaking the fast are obligatory while the other schools hold it to be optional. All schools agree that shortening the prayer applies to the prayers containing four cycles only, that is, the noon, afternoon and evening prayers, while the morning and sunset prayers remain unaltered.

## N – The Eid al-Fitr Prayer

1.  The four schools differ concerning the obligatory or recommended nature of the festival prayer. The Hanafis say that it is an obligation binding upon every individual according to the same conditions as apply to the Friday prayer. If some of the conditions are missing, the necessity of performing the Eid prayer is nullified. The Hanbalis say that the prayer is an obligation upon the community. The obligation of its performance cannot be discharged by the individual alone. The Shafi'i and Maliki school contend that it is a confirmed Prophetic practice (*sunnah*).

2.  According to the Shafi'is the time of the prayer is from the rising of the sun until midday. According to the Hanbalis it is about two hours after sunrise until midday.

3. The Shafi'i school contends that praying alone or in congregation is permissible. Other schools say that it is an obligation to perform the festival prayer in congregation.

4. According to all schools the festival prayer is two cycles done in the following manner:

   a. With the Hanafis, the intention is made first, followed by the magnification (*'Allahu Akbar'*), the same as is required for the daily prayers. After this Allah is then praised, and *'Allahu Akbar'* is repeated three more times. One remains silent after each time for the amount of time it would take to say the *takbir* three times. Then the first chapter of the Qur'an is recited, followed by another chapter. This is followed by bowing (*ruku'*) and two prostrations (*sujud*). The second cycle begins with the first chapter of Qur'an, another chapter and then three magnifications. This is followed by bowing and two prostrations. After this the prayer is completed as normal.

   b. According to the Shafi'is, the prayer begins with *'Allahu Akbar'*, the same as any other prayer. A supplication then follows, after which the *takbir* is said seven times in between which a supplication is repeated silently. One then petitions Allah for refuge from Shaytan and recites the first chapter of the Qur'an followed by the chapter entitled al-Qaf. The bowing and two prostrations are then performed and one should then stand for the second cycle, saying *'Allahu Akbar'* while rising. In the second cycle the takbir (*'Allahu Akbar'*) is said five times and after each one a supplication is made as in the first cycle. Then the first chapter of the Qur'an and the chapter entitled al-Ghashiyah are recited, whereafter the prayer is completed as usual.

c.  According to the Hanbalis, the magnification (*takbir*), which is obligatory at the start of the prayer, is pronounced followed by the recitation of a particular supplication. Then '*Allahu Akbar*' is repeated six times, while between each one a phrase in remembrance of Allah is said silently, whereafter one takes refuge from the devil by reciting the opening chapter of the Qur'an and the chapter al-A'la. Then one completes the first cycle as usual and resumes the standing posture for the second cycle, saying the *takbir*. In the second cycle the *takbir* is recited five times and the phrase mentioned before is repeated after each time. One then recites the opening chapter of the Qur'an followed by the Surah al-Ghashiyah, and completes the prayer in the normal fashion.

d.  According to the Malikis the obligatory magnification begins the prayer and is followed by six repetitions of '*Allahu Akbar*', the recitation of the opening chapter of the Qur'an and Surah al-A'la. The rest of the cycle is performed as normal and one resumes the standing posture while saying the takbir. In the second cycle five repetitions of '*Allahu Akbar*' are followed by the recitation of the opening chapter of the Qur'an and Surah ash-Shams, or any other Surah one may choose to recite. The remainder of the prayer is completed in the usual way.

## O - Alms

The alms given at the end of Ramadan is also called the 'alms of the individual' (*zakat ul-fitr*).

1.  The four schools say that giving the alms is binding upon every capable Muslim, young or old. The guardian of a child or an unstable person is responsible for the payment of alms from their own wealth.

2. According to the Hanafis the capable Muslim is one who possesses a portion of wealth upon which the wealth tax (*zakat*) may be levied, or the value of his wealth is in excess of his needs. The Shafi'is, Malikis and Hanbalis say that the capable one is he who finds that what he has provided for both himself and his family is in excess of his needs on the night or during the day of the festival. This does not include what he needs for housing, clothing and necessary household items. The Malikis add that if someone is able to get a loan, knowing that he can repay it when it is due, he is considered capable.

3. The Hanafis say that it is an obligation for the capable individual to pay the alms for himself, his children, and servants, as well as any older children that are mad. As for older children of sound mind, the father is not required to pay for them. The husband is not obliged to pay the alms required of his wife.

   The Hanbalis and Shafi'i is say that a person is obliged to pay alms for himself and his dependents, such as his wife, children and elders or indigent parents. The Malikis say that it is an obligation to pay alms for oneself and whomever he is responsible for supporting, such as his parents when they are poor, male children who have no money until they be mature and are able to earn an income for themselves, daughters until they marry, and his wife.

4. All schools save for the Hanafis agree that the amount which is obligatory for each person to pay is 3 kilograms or 6.6 lbs of either wheat, barley, dates, raisins, rice, corn or whatever is usually eaten. The Hanafis say it is sufficient to give 1.5 kilograms of wheat.

5. Hanafis say that the time of the obligation is from the dawn of the festival day until the last day of one's life. The obligation is flexible and can be given in advance or later. The Hanbalis hold that it is forbidden to delay the payment of alms until after the festival. Payment can be made two days before the

Eid celebration but not earlier. The Shafi'is contend that the time of payment is from sunset of the last day of Ramadan until sunset of Eid. It is forbidden to pay it after the sunset of the festival day, unless there be a very particular reason. The Malikis hold that it is due at sunset on the last day of Ramadan.

6.  The schools agree that those who deserve the alms are the ones who deserve the general alms of wealth, as mentioned in the verse of the Qur'an, 'Charity is for the poor and the destitute.'

7.  Payment according to the price of the grain instead of the grain itself is acceptable. Payment to poor relatives first is preferred, then to poor neighbours, according to the tradition, 'Neighbours deserve charity more than others.'

# Chapter Seven

## Supplication and Worship During Ramadan

Supplication to the Lord and seeking His help and guidance is a most important element of worship during the month of Ramadan. The needs for which one may supplicate range from existential and worldly aspects to subtler and higher aspirations. Supplication is the expression of needs which vary in quantity and quality. The priority moves from the material and physical to the mental and intellectual towards a higher and subtler condition of an illumined heart.

Ultimately the seeker's greatest desire is to be in a state of constant illumination, awareness and purity of heart. With sincere worship a point is reached where there is no need for outer expression in the form of language. The constant recognition of the all-pervasive Light and Power of Allah suffices. From this comes the recognition that humanity itself only exists in order to worship and know its source, the exalted Lord of all creation. Natural needs and desires exist in order to lead us to the root of fulfilment, which is the Divine Presence whose light shines in the contented heart. Guidance and appropriate action or inaction follows from this healthy spiritual state.

Life is based on interaction, change and the fulfilment of numerous needs. Nature will ensure that one experiences numerous deisres, wishes and needs so as to drive one towards their fulfilment. The fewer these desires, the greater the likelihood of attaining contentment and inner peace.

Since the time when the final message of Islam crystallized through the prophethood of Muhammad, Muslims have gathered and used the many supplications and other special prayers used for different occasions throughout the year. Most of these supplications and other extra acts of worship can be traced back to the Prophet and his Household and Companions, may the peace and blessings of Allah be upon them all. The following selection is a small taste of those supplications that relate to Ramadan.

O Most High, Most Mighty, Forgiving and Merciful, there is no one like you, the One Who hears and sees all. You have magnified, ennobled, honoured and preferred this month over all other months. In this month You have made fasting obligatory for me, and in this month You sent down the Qur'an as a guidance to all people, a clear explanation, and a criterion between what is good and what is evil. You made the Night of Determination, in which you sent it down, excel a thousand months.

O Possessor of boundless generosity to Whom no one can be generous, be generous to me by allowing me freedom from the fire. Allow me to enter the Garden by Your mercy, O Most Merciful of those who show mercy.

\*\*\*\*\*

The following prayer is recommended after every obligatory *salat*:

O Allah, cause enduring joy to enter the people of the graves. Enrich everyone who is contented with little. Absolve the debt of everyone who is indebted.

O Allah, bring joy to everyone who is saddened. Return the stranger in a strange land to his home.

O Allah, correct what is corrupt amongst the affairs of the Muslims. Cure every sick one and enrich our poverty with Your wealth.

O Allah, change the inappropriateness of our state with the excellence of Your state. Absolve our debts and bring us into a state of complete dependence upon You, for You are Powerful over all things.

\*\*\*\*\*

The Supplication of Pilgrimage was often recited during Ramadan by Imam al-Sadiq, especially after the sunset prayer:

> O Allah, by You and from You I seek what I need. Who is it that seeks what he needs from people? I seek what I need from You alone, for You have no partner. By Your overflowing grace I ask for blessings upon the Prophet Muhammad and the people of his house. Make a way for me to Your Sacred House with an accepted Pilgrimage, one that is purified and performed sincerely for You; one by which my state will be exalted. Allow me to be among those whose glance is cast down and whose purity is upheld, so that by this pilgrimage I shall be able to repel all of the things which are forbidden until there be nothing more beloved to me than obedience to You, fear before You and acting upon that which You love. Allow this, as well as everything that You have bestowed upon me, to happen in ease and well-being. I ask that You allow me to die in Your way amongst Your elite, under the banner of Your Messenger. I ask that you make me an instrument for the downfall of Your enemies and the enemies of Your Messenger. I ask You to ennoble me by that which is worthy of abasement and not to abase me by that which is worthy of ennoblement. O Allah, I ask that You allow me to walk the path of Your Messenger. You, O Lord, are sufficient for me; Your will be done.

*****

Reading the Qur'an either during the day or at night during Ramadan is considered to be the best of actions. It should be read often, with humility and sincerity. For everything there is a spring and the springtime of the Qur'an is Ramadan.

During every month of the year it is Prophetic practice to complete a reading of the whole Qur'an, and this is all the more encouraged in Ramadan. Some of the great saints are known to have read the Qur'an forty times or more during Ramadan, but it is better to read less with understanding than to read a lot mechanically. To benefit fully from reading the Qur'an, one must understand the meaning and then apply the message with a sense of urgency. The key is to be spiritually informed so as to become transformed.

One should frequently recite 'There is no god but Allah'. Imam 'Ali ibn al-Husayn would spend the entire month of Ramadan only in supplication, glorification, seeking forgiveness and magnification of Allah. While ordinarily it is the night that is reserved for extra prayers and supplications, during Ramadan the day becomes as important a time as the night.

The following are three short supplications to recite during Ramadan:

> O Allah! bring the new moon upon us with security, faith, peace, submission and success (for us) to perform that which you love and accept.

*****

> O Allah, keep me secure and at peace in Ramadan and grant me the benefits of Ramadan.

*****

> Allah is Most Great. There is no power or might but from Allah. O Allah, I ask you to grant me the best that there is in this month and I seek refuge in You from the evils of the Determination and the evils of the Day of Resurrection.

## PRAYER

During the month of fasting it is recommended to perform 1000 cycles of prayers (*tarawih*) throughout the month at night. Our Prophetic tradition states that one should do 20 *rak'at* each night after the evening prayer, in groups of two, during the first 20 days of Ramadan. In the last ten days of Ramadan 30 cycles are to be done every night. The 300 cycles which remain are divided between the 19th, 21st, and 23rds nights, at 100 cycles a night. One may recite the following supplication after every two cycles of the *tarawih* prayers:

O Allah, decree for me on the Night of Determination a pilgrimage to Your Sacred House that is worthy of Your praise and decree for me efforts whose wrong actions are forgiven. I ask that You lengthen my years in obedience to You and grant me sustenance from Your abundance. O Lord, You are the Most Merciful of the Merciful.

Supplication and prayers during the fast of Ramadan heighten the awareness of human weakness, humility and dependence on Allah for success in all matters. Adoration and worship of the One reduces the natural illusion of dependency and importance of worldly creations and relationships.

# Chapter Eight

# The Night of Determination *(Laylat al-Qadar)*

The Qur'an was revealed to the Prophet Muhammad in one instant, in a condensed flash of timeless illumination on what we know as 'the Night of Determination or Decree' *(Laylat al-Qadr)*, one of the unevenly numbered days during the last ten days of Ramadan. Existentially, however, the Qur'an was unfolded through sound and the world of time and space over a period of twenty three years. The transformative nature of the Qur'an initiated a physical, mental and spiritual revolution which first affected those closest to the Prophet, then radiated out into Arab society and finally extended throughout the world. This pattern of instantaneous revelation, followed by a gradual unfoldment, is a model that had occurred several times before Muhammad with earlier great prophets.

The Qur'an reveals the universal pattern and map of all creational realities, seen and unseen. The Qur'an is the bridge between the zone of timeless and spaceless dominion and the realm of creational existence. The person fasting seeks to draw near in knowledge, understanding and sensitivity to the source and light of the revealed Qur'an.

The purpose of fasting in Ramadan is contained in the meaning of the Night of Determination. The secret of the Night of Determination relates to Allah's Powers and Presence in this world as well as beyond time and space. To be a Muslim is to live the Qur'an, to live a transformed way of life based on subtle awareness and deep knowledge.

Revelation and Divine Mercy are unquestionably associated with fasting, solitude and abstention from personal and social disturbances and natural interactions. Moses fasted in solitude on Mount Sinai for 40 days before receiving the revelation of the Torah, and Jesus fasted alone in the desert for 40 days before his prophethood to the Children of Israel. The Prophet Muhammad took to the cave in Mount Hira during the month of Ramadan, which was the traditional month of retreat for the spiritually inclined descendants of the Prophet Ishmael. It is also quite likely that he had fasted whilst in retreat. It was during his isolation in the cave that the Qur'an was revealed to him, as we are told in Surat al-Baqarah (The Cow):

> The month of Ramadan [is that] in which the Qur'an was revealed. (2:185)

The actual event of the revelation took place on the Night of Determination – also known in translation as the Night of Power – as Allah reveals to us in the Surah of the same name:

> In the name of Allah, the Compassionate, the Merciful.
>
> Surely We have revealed it on the Night of Determination.
>
> And what will cause you to comprehend the Night of Determination?
>
> The Night of Determination is better than a thousand months.
>
> In it descend the Angels and the Spirit by the permission of their Lord – empowered for every affair – Peace! it is until the break of dawn. (97:1-5)

And:

> And the Clear Book. Surely We have caused it to descend in a blessed night. (44:5)

From these verses we infer that the inner revelation to the Prophet occurred all at once, while the outer revelation was apportioned, according to the appropriate circumstances, over a period of twenty three years, as the following verses prove:

> A Qur'an that We have revealed in portions, that you may recite it to the people by slow degrees. (17:106)

Those who disbelieve say: Why was the Qur'an not revealed to
him all at once? Thus, that We may strengthen your heart by it
and We have arranged it well. (25:32)

Allah named this night the Night of Determination (or Power, or
Measure) as an indication of its importance and power to
determine the events of the coming year, such as life, death,
provision, happiness and misfortune. This He established by His
words:

Therein every wise affair is made distinct, a command from Us.
Surely We are the Messengers, a mercy from your Lord. (44:4-
6)

The phrase 'every wise affair is made distinct' means the precise
execution of how particular events are decreed or determined. All
events unfold through time according to changing conditions, but
still subject to Allah's Laws which govern the entire creation. The
events of a future year are conceived at one time yet unfold
according to the changing circumstances and conditions of the
physical realm in which they materialize. These events manifest
gradually through a chain of cause and effect. Individual destiny,
however, is subject to being exposed to different sets of decrees
and events.

*Laylat al-Qadr* recurs every year. What establishes this fact is
the use of the imperfect tense in the relevant verses, which
indicates the ongoing nature of the event. Thus in the verses 'The
Night of Determination is better...'and 'The Angels and the Spirit
descend in it...', both the verbs translated here as 'is' and 'descend'
are in the imperfect past tense in the Arabic. Some enlightened
Muslims explain 'Determination' to mean the station or standing
(*maqam*) of those who worship in it.

Creation, the realm of manifestation of substance, energy and
events, is in constant flux, moving cyclically through upsurges and
downswings. Thus it stands to reason that there is one night within
a period of time when the creational energies are at their most
powerful. As on a macrocosmic scale, man as a microcosm also
has his periods of greater or lesser strength, tranquillity or peace.

If a human being's zenith of inner containment and peace coincides with the annual cosmic event, he will have tasted an aspect of understanding the inner meaning of the Decree and Destiny.

The continuing fast and other spiritual practices, obligatory and recommended, that are prescribed for the month of Ramadan prepare the seeker for the Night of Determination. By then the sincere seeker will be at the peak of sensitivity, awareness and spiritual health. 'The Night of Determination' will mark full faith, surrender and high expectations of Allah for the prepared seeker.

Allah says: 'And what will cause you to understand what the Night of Determination is?' Throughout the Qur'an such rhetorical questions serve to emphasize the importance and significance of what is being mentioned. Here the verse alludes to the majesty and sublimity of this special night. The next verse confirms this uniqueness: 'The Night of Determination is better than a thousand months'. Thus this exalted position confers on the seeker's worship a thousand-fold increase in value and effectiveness.

When we come to know something, we realize that the state of this knowledge is better than the many previous years of ignorance. In a period of ten years we may remember two or three days that were critical, which contained those moments that changed the entire course of our lives and the way we perceived things. Those days are naturally charged with far greater significance than a thousand months. Because the nature of Truth is eternal, any reflected beams of its Light will always overcome darkness and cut through time.

Allah says: 'The Angels and the Spirit descend therein by permission of their Lord'. What is pp pqpd as Spi r it ( *ruh*) here is closely related in Arabic to the word for 'breeze, wind or breath'. Spirit is subtle, palpable but intangible. The spirit is a Divine Breeze which is blown into the body and later blown out of it. The Qur'an says:

They ask you about the Spirit. Say: the Spirit is from the command of my Lord.  (17:85)

On the Night of Determination the All-Mighty, All-Powerful Lord extends His mercy and opens up the skies. The angelic powers fulfil their merciful duty of bringing forth the unifying Divine Light directly from its source.

The very last phrase, 'for every affair', could also be read as 'pertaining to every affair'. The verse can therefore be read as follows: 'The Angels and Spirit descend in it by the permission of their Lord pertaining to every affair.' Both are correct. The descent originates from the Divine Command and through the vehicle of the spirit, that subtle energy which vivifies and animates every affair.

'Peace! it is until the break of dawn': from the knowledge that all creation exists according to decrees and measures and is moving toward a destiny in conformity with these comes the peace of certainty. This inner certainty, which illumines all possible outer manifestations, brings about a state of trust, equilibrium and balance that in turn renders the awakened being bewildered in harmony and unity. The meaning of that peace, which is the result of knowledge, is inherent in every heart. For this seed to grow and bear fruit the heart must be purified and opened up to confirm these subtle mercies.

Whoever seeks knowledge of Allah spends his days and nights awaiting the moment of real openings, and when that occurs it is like the crack of dawn. The state of the heart of the one gifted with Divine Knowledge is hidden in the darkness of the night but is inwardly illumined. Outwardly it is quiet but inwardly it is active and dynamic, absorbed in the sea of Gnosis. The root of everything lies in its opposite. Most spiritual progress often occurs late at night until dawn, when outwardly there is least physical action and therefore a maximum possibility for inner sensitivity and awareness to predominate.

# TRADITIONS CONCERNING 'THE NIGHT OF DETERMINATION'

1. The Prophet was asked by Abu Dharr if the Night of Determination was only in the time of the Prophets. He replied, 'No, it will continue until the Day of Reckoning.'

2. The Prophet said:

   On the Night of Determination the angels who reside at the Lote Tree of the Uttermost Boundary descend. Amongst them is Gabriel who raises a standard upon my grave, the holy mosque in Jerusalem, the mosque surrounding the Ka'bah and upon Mount Sinai.

3. The Prophet was asked about the Night of Determination. He stood up to answer, and after thanking and glorifying Allah, he said:

   You have asked me [before] about the Night of Determination. I did not keep it from you because I did not have knowledge of it. Know, O people, that whoever witnesses Ramadan and is well, fastings its days and worshipping part of its nights, keeping its prayers and attending its Fridays, and meeting its festival, has reached the Night of Determination and won the great gift of his Lord.

   Commenting upon this tradition, Imam al-Sadiq said, 'He has won by Allah, with great gifts which are not the same as the gifts of the ordinary human being.'

4. Imam al-Sadiq also said:

   The Determination occurs on the 19th, its confirmation is on the 21st and its completion is on the 23rd night of the month of Ramadan.

5. Imam al-Sadiq was asked by a group of people whether blessings and sustenance are apportioned during the night of the 15th of Sha'ban (the month preceding Ramadan), as was commonly believed before Islam. He said:

   No, by Allah, this event does not occur except on the 19th, 21st and 23rd of Ramadan. On the night of the 19th the two gatherings meet, on the night of the 21st every judicious affair is distinguished, and on the night of the 23rd what Allah willed is completed, and it is the Night of Determination of which Allah spoke when He said: "Better than a thousand months".

A man then asked the Imam what the phrase 'the two gatherings meet' meant. The Imam replied:

Allah gathers what He has willed with that which He sent forward and that which has been held back. Thus does He will and execute destiny.

The man then asked him what was the meaning of 'He completes it on the 23rd.' The Imam said:

The difference between the 21st night and the 23rd is that on the 21st the affair is drawn out and on the 23rd it is accomplished and becomes definite.

6.  A man once asked Imam al-Sadiq about the verse: 'Surely We have revealed it on a blessed night.' The Imam explained:

It is the Night of Determination which occurs every year in the month of Ramadan during the last ten days. Allah has said: "In it every judicious matter is distinguished". During the Night of Determination, whatever is to occur is decreed for the coming year, concerning good and evil, obedience and disobedience, birth, death and provision. Whatever was decreed for that year and comes to pass was decisively determined, and Allah, the Mighty and Majestic, is the One Whose will it is that brings it to pass.

The man continued with his question, 'What does "the Night of Determination is better than a thousand months" mean?' The Imam replied:

Good actions such as the prayer, charity, and other things during Ramadan are worth the actions of a thousand other months.

7.  Imam al-Sadiq was asked by a man named Zararah about the Night of Determination and he replied, 'It is the night of the 21st or the 23rd.' Zararah then asked, 'Is it not only one

night?' The Imam replied, 'Yes.' Zararah then said, 'Please tell me which one it is.' 'You must do good in both nights,' the Imam replied.

8. Imam al-Sadiq was asked about Allah's wisdom: 'Surely We have revealed it on a blessed night'. He said:

> It means the Night of Determination and it occurs every year during the month of Ramadan in the last ten days. The Qur'an was revealed on the Night of Determination. Allah says about it: "In it every wise affair is distinguished."

9. Imam al-Sadiq also said about the Night of Determination:

> Everything that is to happen in the coming year is decreed on the Night of Determination, including the good, the bad, obedience, disobedience, birth, death, and one's provision. Whatever is decreed in this night with finality will inevitably come to pass. Allah discharges His power so that He does what He wills.

10. When Imam al-Sadiq was asked whether the angel Gabriel and the Spirit were the same he replied:

> Gabriel is an angel and the Spirit is greater than the angels. They are not the same, for Allah distinguished between the two of them when He said "The Angels and the Spirit descend in it by the permission of their Lord."

The sincere seeker prepares himself or herself for *Laylat al-Qadr* by outer restriction regarding worldly interaction, as confirmed by performing *ghusl* and passing the night in prayer, supplication and reading of the Qur'an, so as to bring himself or herself into a heightened state of submission and inner abandonment. The greater and deeper the submission, the more profound the effect of this glorious night of spiritual power and unveiling.

# Chapter Nine

# The Inner Meaning of Fasting

As the spirit is to the body, so are the inner meanings to the outer practices of Islam. The body has no life without the spirit and the spirit has no expression without the body. Thus, every form of worship has an external and an internal dimension, each of which has its different facets and degrees. Human beings cannot remain content with the shell for they need to explore and understand the meaning and essence behind form.

The Messenger of Allah said:

> The root of Islam is prayer (*salat*), its branches are the obiigatory tax (*zakat*), its height is the fast (*sawm*) and its breadth is striving in the way of Allah (*jihad*).

He also said:

> Fasting is half of patience; there is *zakat* for everything and the *zakat* for the body is fasting.

Through fasting one learns tolerance and patience. When the Prophet tells us that the *zakat* of the body is fasting, he means that for the wholesome health of the body fasting is like giving alms to your own body, by giving it a chance to detoxify and be restored to its natural balance.

Imam al-Sadiq relates that the Prophet said:

> The fast is a shield, that is, a veil protecting one from the disturbance of the world and from the punishment of the Hereafter. Thus, when you fast, make the intention to restrain ourselves from its desires and cut off the thoughts inspired by Shaytan. Bring yourself to the place where you are content without the desire for food and drink.

Sayyid Haydar 'Amuli wrote:

> The purpose of the fast is to reduce the desires of the self; it is a
> cleansing for the heart and the body and a revival of both the
> inner and the outer. It also includes gratitude for the grace and
> goodness given by those who stand in need before Allah. It
> increases humility, meekness, and tears, and causes one to seek
> refuge with Allah.

A person's state of beingness is the product of absorption,
consumption and internalisation of his environment. Everything
one experiences through the senses becomes a part of one and
nourishes one as blood nourishes the body. The Prophet had said
that Shaytan flows in the son of Adam in the same way as his
blood, and that the way to constrict his passage was through
fasting, or hunger. In order to experience higher levels of
consciousness one must cut, reduce, or restrict the baser sensory
experiences.

Abu Hamid al-Ghazali said:

> Fasting specifically curbs Shaytan, blocks his ways and
> constricts his passages to the heart of man. Therefore it deserves
> a special relationship to Allah, because it gives victory to Allah.
> Allah's victory for His slave is dependent upon the slave giving
> victory to Allah. For Allah says: "If you give victory to Allah,
> Allah will give you victory and make your feet firm." (47:7).
> Giving to Allah is done by one's own exertion and effort, and
> the reward is right guidance from Allah. Therefore He said: "For
> those who exert themselves for Us We will guide them to our
> ways." (29:69).

Change can only occur by breaking desires. They are the breeding
grounds of the satanic energies where they roam and feed. As long
as the breeding grounds remain fertile, they will not go away but
will increase in strength. Thus Allah says:

> Allah will not change the condition of a people unless they
> change what is in themselves (13:11)

As long as the satanic energies predominate in a person the
Majesty of Allah will not be revealed to the slave and he will

remain veiled from higher consciousness. As the Prophet said: 'If it were not for satanic energies roaming around, surrounding the heart of the son of Adam, he would have readily witnessed the world of the unseen.'

Allah says in the Qur'an:

> Say O my servants who believe! Be careful of (your duty to) your Lord; for those who do good in this world is good, and Allah's earth is spacious. Only the patient will be paid back their reward in full, without measure. (39:10)

All natural phenomena manifest within the realm of opposites. Encompassing this world is a realm 'without measure'. Nature itself is on an expansive, evolutionary course. The manifestation of phenomena in line with this course leads to a multiplication of phenomena which are also in alignment with it. Phenomena which are not in harmony are ultimately rejected by the system. The intensity of the system's reaction to reject an incompatible element is in direct proportion to the strength of an incompatible element. Regarding this the Qur'an says:

> Whoever brings forth that which is suitable has ten of its like, and whoever brings forth evil [what is incompatible] has only [like] recompense. (6:161)

An analogy may be seen in the working of the human body. When it is given good food, fresh air, sanitation and proper exercise it flourishes and functions in a healthy, balanced way. The introduction of bad food, noxious air, unclean living conditions and lack of exercise greatly reduces its capacity for maintaining health and resistance to disease and thus the possibility of illness and loss of equilibrium is increased. The body's reaction to eliminate toxins or germs is in direct proportion to the strength of these undesirable elements combined in relation to the body's overall state of resistance. The body reacts only as much as is necessary to eliminate the incompatible element that is disturbing its balance. The innate course of the body is one of self-sustaining expansion.

Muhsin Fayd al-Kashani wrote:

> Fasting is a screen from the evils of this world and a barrier from
> the punishment of the next. When you fast, make the intention to
> restrain yourself from desires and so sever yourself from the
> plots of the Shaytan by putting yourself in the place of one who
> is sick, desiring neither food nor drink, anticipating at any
> moment to be cured from the illnesses of wrong actions. Purify
> your innermost from any impurity, distraction or darkness which
> cuts you off from the meaning of allegiance to the fact of Allah,
> the Most High.

> Fasting eliminates the elements of the lower self and reduces the
> grip of desires. From it comes purity of heart and faculties,
> wellbeing of the inward and outward, gratitude for blessings,
> beneficence toward the poor, increase in supplication to Allah,
> humility and weeping. Fasting is the rope of taking refuge in
> Allah and the cause for breaking habits and desires. Fasting
> reduces the accounts and multiplies the good deeds. The benefits
> of it are immeasurable. He who has discernment will be aware of
> what we have said and will find success in its use.

> For the men of inner knowledge, the correctness of fasting is its
> acceptability, which depends on whether it has enabled one to
> reach one's objective. They understand that the objective of
> fasting is to take on, as far as possible, the characteristic of self-
> subsistence, which is an Attribute of Allah, the Exalted, and
> which resembles the angels in their lack of desires.

Concerning the meaning of the Prophetic tradition in which the
Messenger of Allah exclaims: 'How many a man fasts while there
is nothing for him in his fasting except hunger and thirst?' Abu
Darda comments:

> How preferable is sleep and the breaking of the fast of the wise
> ones. They will not be cheated like the ignorant in their fasting
> and staying awake. A little bit of inner certainty and piety is far
> better than mountains of worship performed by the arrogant.

Upon reflection one wonders how many people who are fasting are
in actual fact breaking their fast, and how many who appear to be
breaking their fast are actually fasting. The former are those who
keep all their faculties free from errors and sins while eating and

drinking. The latter are those who feel the hunger and thirst of the fast but allow all their senses and faculties to roam rampantly.

Whoever understands the meaning of fasting and its secret will be able to discern the outer and inner realities to fasting. Take, for example, the person who, while fasting, refrains from eating and sexual intercourse, but breaks his fast by committing many mistakes. He is like someone who has washed properly during the ritual purification for prayer, with all the proper courtesy and supplications, but did not perform the major ritual ablution (after intercourse). His prayers will be of little or no benefit to him because he is in darkness and ignorance. As for whoever is not fasting from food but is fasting with all his faculties from wrong actions, it is as if he has washed all his limbs, limiting himself to what is obligatory. His prayers are correct and acceptable according to what is obligatory, even though he may have left out the recommended extra courtesies and supplications. Whoever combines both fasting from food as well as withholding the faculties has united the obligatory with what is recommended, thus rendering the fast complete.

## The Outer Abstentions of Fasting

The outer conditions of fasting cover more than the mere abstention from the intake of sustenance. They also address the abstention of the tongue, eyes, ears, sense of smell, taste, and touch.

The abstention of the tongue relates to useless, foolish or discourteous speech, as well as anything which would be contrary to what pleases Allah. The Prophet said:

Whoever is silent is saved.

He also said:

When the discussion reaches Allah, then be silent.

And:

Whoever knows his Lord, his tongue becomes still.

That is to say, one is incapable of speaking about he greatness of Allah and His Majesty. The tongue is incapable of expressing the inexpressible for the Divine Light burns away all existential lights and shadows.

The Prophet also said:

> Whoever speaks too much, speaks frivolously; whoever speaks frivolously has little modesty; whoever has little modesty has little restraint; and whoever has little restraint enters the Fire.

Abstention of the eye involves restraining one's sight from things which are forbidden to behold as well as abstaining from actions and things which are permitted to the extent of necessity. It is to this which Allah alludes when He tells us:

> Tell the people of faith to keep their glance averted and to guard their private parts. (24:30)

If one does not see something, one's self will neither demand it nor incline towards it. Having never seen colours, the blind man does not recognise the difference between them and therefore has no desire whatsoever to match them up.

Abstention of the ears relates to refraining from hearing whatever Allah has declared to be forbidden, like slander and gossip, forbidden music or singing, and listening to the talk of the misguided and corrupt.

Abstention of the sense of smell refers to both foul odours as well as pleasant scents. Bad odours generate aversion and disgust, while pleasant or sweet scents may arouse desires and the pursuit of outer pleasures.

Abstention of the sense of taste relates to being drawn to desires and veiling the faculty of reason by imbibing intoxicating beverages, or by acquiring a taste for usury and unfair profit, abuse of orphans and the weak, and various other such 'tastes' which are forbidden. Allah says:

> And do not approach the property of the orphan except in the best manner...(6:153)

He also says:

> Those who swallow usury cannot arise except as one whom Shaytan has prostrated by [his] touch. (2:275)

Abstention of the sense of touch is from whatever may lead one to commit forbidden actions or to excesses in permitted actions, and to go beyond the limits of balance. Allah has mentioned this when He said:

> They will say to their skins, "Why have you testified against us?" They will reply, "Allah has caused us to speak, it is He Who gives speech to everything and He created you in the first instance and to Him you will return." (41:21)

He also says:

> You did not veil yourselves lest your ears or your eyes or your skins testify against you. (41:22)

The senses have been created to function responsibly in harmony and balance. Anyone who uses the body and its various parts in a manner for which it was not created is a wrong-doer, because wrong-doing causes an imbalance, which is the exact opposite of harmony and justice.

The Prophet said:

> Five things will break the fast of anyone: Lying, speaking behind people's backs, creating mischief between two people, bearing false witness and looking [upon someone] with lust.

The main objective of fasting is to weaken the senses and reduce distraction and wrong action. This cannot be achieved but by reducing one's intake. Thus the evening meal taken when breaking one's fast should be no more than what would be eaten any normal evening, as though one had not fasted. If while breaking fast one eats all that is usually eaten during the course of a whole day no benefit is gained from the fast. In fact, the courtesy (*adab*) of fasting is such that one should not sleep much during the day so that one tastes hunger and thirst and becomes conscious of one's frailty and weakness.

## The Inner Abstentions of Fasting

Inner abstention is the usual practice maintained by serious people on the path of spiritual discipline. During fasting it is the core of their continued and heightened spiritual practice. Fasting merely stimulates and accentuates sensitivity and awareness. Abstentions of the inner include the following:

1. Restraining the faculty of thought and intellect from being used for affairs that are not apt, necessary or appropriate, for the Prophet said with regard to this faculty:

   The reflection of an hour is better than the actions of seventy years.

2. Restraining the power of imagination so that the true nature of things is not veiled by illusion and fantasy. Allah created the faculty of imagination as a screen for the physical world, which is a realm of allegory and representation. Everything in the higher, spiritual world is mirrored and shadowed in the lower world of form. For example, the light of the sun represents Divine Light. The thickest veil of the self is its continuous shifting back and forth from the physical form to meaning.

Shaykh Muhyi al-Din ibn al-'Arabi said:

   Know that the eyes, ears, tongue, hands, stomach, private parts and the feet are man's workers and his authorised agents. Each one of them is an administrator and disburser of the wealth it oversees. The leader of all the authorised agents is sensory perception, which all of the senses resort to through its agent. Sensory perception, in its leadership and domination, is subordinate to the authority of idealisational imagination which, in turn, in both its capacity for good and bad, is subordinate to the authority of reflection, which is under the control of the intellect. The intellect is the minister of man.

Regarding the intellect Shaykh Mir Muttalib says:

   Praise belongs to Allah, He who is clothed by Eternal Divinity and is unique in oneness that has no beginning and no end. He made the intellect a drop from the kingdom of the unseen forms, the kingdom of the source-forms of creational realities.

Shaykh ibn al-'Arabi says that if the faculty of imagination is able to shift freely between meaning and form without restraint, then it is not subordinate to awareness and reflection. Shifting to and fro does not allow for unification, which is the goal of the spiritual path – to see one first and then experience two.

3. Restraining the capacity of illusion (of values) which in one instant represents one's repulsion and in the next attraction. The self is thus prevented from being steadfast and just, which is unity in the true sense, because it falls prey to transient feelings of affection and enmity. Through restraint of the capacity of illusion or subjective perception, the lower aspect of the self co-operates with, and supports, the faculties of anger and desire. The opposite, higher aspect of the self is contentment of being, in which one witnesses the Beloved and His dominions. The awakened self feels no enmity or affection toward anyone, for it is free, simply witnessing the one and only Reality. This station has been described by Allah:

Say: Allah! Then leave them to dally in their idle discussion (6:6)

The one who possesses a 'tranquil soul' (al-nafs al-mutma'innah) is free of all this since he is in the station of witnessing the Beloved, and 'anything the Beloved does is loved.'

4. Restraining sensory perception from participating with imagination and illusion in the presentation of form and meaning to the self. Anyone who is preoccupied with physical form is veiled from meaning and spirituality, and anyone who is occupied with illusory meanings is veiled from the meanings of manifesting reality. The one who is veiled is veiled, whether by one veil or a thousand. One who fasts must restrain himself from this situation and be liberated from all the veils, while witnessing the Beloved in all facets.

The self may be likened to a tree that has ten branches, each one taking its nourishment from the trunk. If nine branches be cut off, then the energy and nourishment allotted to them would go to the remaining branch. Thus it would flourish and increase in size, yielding larger, finer and healthier fruit. So it is with the self. If man cuts off his attachment to the surrounding world and attaches himself to none branch, there is not doubt that the fruit of reflection will be higher, greater, subtler and nobler.

5. Restraining the heart from feeling confident that one's fast has been accepted. Upon breaking the fast, the heart must remain between fear and hope because one does not know whether one's fast has been accepted or not. This humble uncertainly should be one's state after every act of worship.

He who desires to see One must in all circumstances restrain himself from seeing actions as emanating from other than Allah. This is called the station of the unity of actions (*tawhid al-af'al*). Then it is necessary that he restrain himself from seeing attributes other than those of Allah, so that he may reach the station of the unity of Attributes (*tawhid al-sifat*). And finally, he must abstain from seeing other than the constant presence of Allah. That is the station of the unity of Essence (*tawhid al-dhat*). This final station is the goal of the Spiritual Path. Whoever reaches this degree, even if he intends to see other than Allah he would not be able to do so. The tongue of his state would say: 'If a desire other than You occurred to me, by this false notion I judge myself out of Islam.'

The ultimate objective of the Path is to reach the abode of seeing the One Source behind multiple manifestations, otherwise one is a *mushrik* (idolator, seeing other than Allah). Prayer and fasting are basically the cleansing of the inner from the impurity of associating others with Allah, and from the illusion of the grossness of 'otherness' by the water of Unity and the light of faith based upon knowledge. In prayer and other acts of worship one cannot cleanse the inner unless one cleanses the outer by way of *wudu'* and *ghusl*. Similarly the fast is not valid for the *mushrik*, whether his *shirk* be open or concealed, because every *mushrik* or *kafir* is one who rejects the Absolute Truth, as Allah says:

> And whoever associates [others] with Allah has indeed gone far astray. (4:116)

Allah alludes to concealed *shirk* in the following verse:

> Thus whoever seeks to meet his Lord then let him do good actions and not associate anyone in the worship of his Lord. (18:110)

If the reference is for open *shirk*, the verse would have said: '...and not associate anyone with his Lord.' But when He says, 'in the worship of his Lord', it implies one who secretly associates others with Allah, who are referred to as 'believers' or 'Muslims', as Allah says:

> And most of them do not believe in Allah without associating [others with Him]. (12:102)

And the Prophet said:

> The infiltration of *shirk* among my people is more hidden than the creeping of a black ant upon a black stone in the pitch black of night.

Whoever fasts and consequently abstains from anything other than Allah is fasting according to the following *hadith qudsi*:

> For every good action there is the recompenses of ten to seven hundred times its worth, except fasting, for indeed, it is solely for Me and I am its reward.

Everything other than this type of fast does not deserve a reward of this magnitude. Fasting is a means for refining the behaviour and for assuming the Attributes of Allah, as the Prophet said:

> Mould yourselves with the high moral attributes which are Allah's.

Fasting is ultimately a means of attaining annihilation and cleansing of the self by Allah in the station of Pure Unity, which is referred to as 'annihilation in Unity'; as Allah says in a *hadith qudsi*:

> Whoever has sought after Me has found Me. Whoever has found Me has come to know Me. Whoever has known Me has loved Me. Whoever has loved Me I have slain. Whomever I have slain, the payment of the blood-wit is due from Me, and I Myself will be the payment for the blood-wit owed.

Some of those who know Allah have provided the following subtle analogy using fire and coal. Fire is characterised by brightness, burning and heat, while coal is a substance which possesses the opposite characteristics of darkness, opacity and absence of heat. When coal is placed in or close to a fire it gradually begins to take on all the characteristics of the fire, that is, it starts to glow. The coal then becomes the fire and fire emanates from the coal.

> Those are analogies We provide for mankind, and they will only be understood by those who know. (29:43)

# Conclusion

Fasting is a religious exercise for the whole of one's being – mind, body and soul. It is an obligation by which Allah is remembered and worshipped, and which brings about proximity between the realms of matter and spirit. The human body is a complex material creation whose substances naturally incline toward physical decay and degeneration. If man is to attain a higher state of spiritual consciousness and growth, it is essential that he restrict and control the lower nature of the self and its desires and attachments. By restricting the physical and lower elements of the self we enhance the higher and Divinely guided facets within us. After a few days of continuous fasting the chemical and hormonal patterns of the body changes and this disturbance is the rhythm continues until one is somewhat confused outwardly. This state makes it easy for one to have a shift in old perceptions and values.

Hunger and thirst are basically the spirit and secret of fasting. By abstention we learn how to restrain the self and restrict its demands. Denying the passions of the lower self, the *nafs,* is a major purpose of the fast, whereby the seeker is brought closer to the source and root of life within.

In Islam, the fast of Ramadan is not just a ritualistic, ceremonial period during which the Qur'an was revealed to the Prophet as a code of conduct and the means of salvation. Fasting the month of Ramadan is a major discipline on the road of personal spiritual transformation.

Fasting purifies the body, while leaving the mind acutely receptive to meanings and attributes of outer stimuli and events. It was in such a heightened state of awareness that the Prophet Muhammad received the revelation of the Qur'an. Long before the advent of full prophethood, Muhammad regularly went into spiritual retreat for weeks at a time, usually in the cave of Mount

Hira. Since no once can be certain as to precisely on which of the last ten nights of Ramadan the Night of Determination falls, Muslims retreat for these ten night to a mosque, in imitation of the Prophetic practice.

'Fasting is prescribed for you as it was for those before you.' (2:183) For the Christians fasting was a penitential exercise (the Lenten abstinence), but for the Jews it had an atoning function (Yom Kippur means 'Day of Atonement'). Muslims fast Ramadan as a total act of worship, dedication, submission and prayer for knowledge of Allah and His ways. Fasting can, however, be undertaken at other times as an expiation or compensation (*kaffarah*) for sins and errors. The fast of Ramadan is also penitential in character, as exemplified in the practice of retreat.

The personal spiritual benefits that fasting generate are obvious, but the social benefits are equally significant. Both the Arabic terms from fasting, *sawm* and *siyam*, are from the root meaning 'to be at rest; to abstain, to elevate. The word also implies patience and silence. Thus when Maryam is instructed by Allah (19:26) to say that she has vowed unto the Beneficent a fast and may not speak this day with any mortal, it means she undertook fasting from speech.

The fast of Ramadan is one of the fundamental practices of Islam – the others being prayer, payment of *zakat*, pilgrimage and *jihad*. The last three are of a social character in that they bring the whole community into better harmony and understanding. Charity is where every individual gives alms in remembrance of the one Give, Allah. Pilgrimage is where routine everyday life is left behind so as to seek knowledge of the One Sustainer-Creator, and where prince and pauper stand shoulder to shoulder, clad in the same garb. *Jihad* is to strive to the utmost of one's abilities, both outwardly and inwardly, against the lower tendencies so as to awaken to our higher light within. *Jihad* is ever-continuous. But while both prayer and fasting are essentially private acts of worship that have an immediate effect on the practitioner, they also promote unity of the *ummah*. Prayer is, after all, where the community stands together, shoulder to shoulder, in obedience to Allah.

The shared experience of fasting, breaking the fast and celebrating the Eid promotes the cohesion of the community and unites its direction in life. The successful completion of the month of fasting is a personal triumph for the individual, but one which is shared on the Eid al-Fitr with others. While Eid al-Fitr marks the end of Ramadan, Eid al-Adha likewise marks the successful completion of the Pilgrimage. Both celebrate critical events: the latter the redemption of the prophet Isma'il, progenitor of the line of the Prophet Muhammad, the former the descent upon Muhammad of Allah's final, clear and definitive revelation. In this sense Eid al-Fitr stands worlds apart from the 'carnival' that precedes Lent (carnival is from the Latin: *carne vale*, meaning 'farewell to flesh'). While 'carnival' gives free rein to worldly appetites before their restraint during Lent, the Eid, by contrast, moderately readmits those activities that had been restricted during Ramadan after a period of purification and, as it were, rehabilitation. Thus the correct courtesy is not to marry during Ramadan, but to wait until or after the Eid. Eid is set apart by the donning of new garments, the communal Eid prayer and the hospitality shared among friends and family.

The contrast between fasting and feasting revitalises life in a way that is absent from cultures where fasting has lost its full meaning and benefit. The balance between the two in Islam highlights the fact that Islam is the *Din* of harmony and equilibrium. The code of conduct of Islam reflects the harmony of creation and the Creator's Mercy and Love, without denying this world, but acknowledging the Eternal Light which illumines this world and the Hereafter. At the pinnacle of creation stands the Adamic being, constantly struggling in this world, whilst there lies within him a spirit that is beyond the world of time and space. All the Islamic practices, rituals and rules are a means of subduing the lower self, rendering it subservient to the elevating spiritual guidance that is reflected through the purified heart – the ultimate foundation for human contentment and joy.

# Appendix I to Chapter Five

## The Prayer of the Traveller

The conditions of travelling which cause one to abbreviate the prayer also require that one break the fast. We have, therefore, included in this appendix the rules for abbreviating the prayer during travel, according to the school of the Family of the Prophet or Ja'fari Law. The traveller must reduce the prayers comprised of four *rak'at* to two. The dawn (*fajr*) and sunset (*maghrib*) prayers, however, are not shortened.

## Conditions for Abbreviating the Prayer

1. One's journey must be intentional. If one goes without making the intention to travel, say, in search of a lost thing or person, then one does not truncate the prayers, unless one makes the specific intention to travel the required round-trip distance while on the road and then travels that far, even if it is by piecing together the distances. If, however, one has not made the intention to travel the prescribed distance from the very outset, yet the distance was covered, the prayers performed on the outward leg should be full, while those on the return journey should be abbreviated. The prescribed distance is eight *farsakhs*, that is, 24 miles or 45 kilometres. The following apply:

   a. On a broken, discontinuous journey one must abbreviate prayers at the point where 12 miles (or 22.5 kms) or more has been reached, even though the return journey may not be the same distance. This rule applies to journeys of up to ten days' duration.

   b. The distance may be established by knowledge (scientific or otherwise), clear evidence, as well as by common sense.

c. If the traveller doubts whether he has travelled the prescribed distance and shortens his prayers, then discovers that he has not in fact travelled that distance, he must repeat the same prayers in its full form or compensate for it if its time has passed. If, after having performed a complete prayer, he discovers that he has already travelled the prescribed distance he should likewise repeat the prayer in the abbreviated form.

d. When one intends to go further than the permissible distance (12 miles) from one's town, city or place of residence, one shortens the prayer upon reaching a place in which the call to prayer from one's own town cannot be heard, and its buildings and inhabitants are no longer visible. In the case of a large populated area (which may extend in a radius of 12 miles) one should follow what the people of the locality consider to be the end of one locale and the start of another, or the clear demarcations between districts. As a precaution it is best to pray both the full and the abbreviated forms of each prayer.

2. The intention to travel must be maintained. If one makes the intention changes one's mind during the trip and decides not to travel, one should perform full prayers, unless one changed one's mind after having already travelled 12 miles. If the intention of destination is changed from one locale to another, one must still pray the abbreviated form if the legally prescribed distance has been travelled.

3. When passing through one's place of residence or intending to remain in a place for ten days the journey is considered broken, and the obligation to abbreviate the prayer is lifted. If one remains in a place for 30 days and shortens the prayers because of uncertainty as to whether one would remain in that place, one is thereafter obliged to perform the full prayer.

4. The journey must be legally permissible by Islamic Law, in order for the requirement of abbreviation to be valid:

a. If one's journey is motivated by wrongdoing, such as running away from debts or a legal obligation, one should not truncate the prayers.

b. One should not abbreviate the prayers if the purpose or outcome of one's journey is wrongdoing, e.g. a criminal act, or attending a meeting that is unacceptable according to Islamic Law. The same is true if one proceeds by means considered to be forbidden; e.g. travelling in a land that was taken illegally.

c. The wrongdoer must perform the truncated prayers when he returns from that part of the trip in which he was acting improperly, provided that he is still at a distance where abbreviation is required.

d. Whoever travels on a permissible journey then changes his intention during the trip, intending some wrongful act, must perform the full prayers, as long as he remains within the state of wrongdoing.

e. If the journey is for a purpose contrary to Islamic Law and it is discovered later that what one is doing is not in fact illegal, the journey is no longer contrary to the Law and abbreviated prayers must be performed.

5. One must not shorten the prayers if one travels to hunt for pleasure. If, however, it be out of need for food the prayer should be abbreviated.

6. One should have a permanent place of residence if one is to fall under the category of those obliged to truncate their prayers, i.e. one should not be a nomad, mariner or any other type of individual who continuously moves from one place to another.

7. The journey must not be considered a part of one's job, like the journeys made by mariners, drivers, or travelling salesmen (except when their travelling is unconnected with their work).

a. Those who have professions whose work does not usually require them to travel the prescribed distance must abbreviate their prayers when travelling for the sake of their job.

b. When a job requires journeying only part of the year (like a sailor who might only work in the summer time), one should perform the complete prayer while he is working. The same applies to whoever lives in one county and works consistently in another, and the distance between where he lives and his job is the prescribed distance or beyond.

c. In general, if travelling is part of one's profession, complete prayers should be performed while working.

8. Upon returning, the point at which one must resume praying the full prayer is reached when one is able to hear the call to prayer and see the outskirts of one's place of habitation (for definition of which see 1.d).

## Conditions which Break the Journey

The following conditions dispense with the necessity for abbreviating the prayers and requires that the fast be resumed.

1. Passing one's place of residence, defined as follows:

a. One's home, that is, the original residence where one's parents reside or one's birthplace.

b. The location in which one has taken up permanent residence.

c. The location where one owns a house in which one has resided from six consecutive months, although a person may have more than one place of residence at any one time.

2. Making an intention to remain in a specific location for ten consecutive days. Included in this condition is having to

remain by force or under an emergency. The following considerations apply:

a. If the traveller intends to remain for a period of less than ten days and has abbreviated the prayers accordingly but errs in his calculation and remains longer than ten days, he must repeat his prayers in the full form.

b. If a woman travelling arrives at a location where she intends to remain for ten days or more and begins her menstrual cycle before the time elapses, she should pray the complete prayers after she has finished her cycle, even if the time remaining amounts to less than ten days.

c. In the case when one intends to stay in a place but changes one's mind:

   i. If complete prayers were being performed before, one continues to perform them in full so long as one remains in that place.

   ii. Abbreviated prayers must be performed if the complete form of the obligatory *rak'ah* prayer had not yet been prayed.

   iii. If one changes one's mind during the prayer before the third cycle, one should shorten the prayer. If one does not do so, the prayer will be invalid and must be repeated in the abbreviated form.

   iv. The ten days must be consecutive, and the first or last nights are not counted.

3. After 30 complete days a traveller who has remained indecisive about staying in a specific location or leaving, without having started a new journey, must perform complete prayers. If he leaves the specific location and travels less than the prescribed distance (12 miles), this does not negate the 30 days spent in uncertainty.

# Appendix II to Chapter Six

## Conditions for Shortening the Prayer:

1. According to the Hanafi school, travelling a distance of 121 kilometres (or 75 miles) round-trip requires shortening the prayers.

   The Maliki, Hanbali, and Shafiʻi schools say that the distance is 81 kilometres (or 50 miles) in one direction only. The Hanbalis and Shafiʻis say there is no harm if the distance is shorter by two miles. The Malikis say that no harm is done if it is shorter by eight miles.

2. One must make an intention to travel beyond the limit. Whoever follows the person who makes such an intention, such as a wife, a servant, a prisoner or a soldier, also follows this intention, provided it is known to them. If it be unknown to them they continue to perform the full prayers.

3. Truncating the prayer is not permitted until after departure from the built-up area of the place of habitation.

4. The journey must be permissible. For example, if one's travel be for the purpose of a forbidden act like stealing one may not shorten the prayers. All agree upon this except the Hanafis who say that one must abbreviate no matter what the purpose of one's travel is, for one will be punished for forbidden acts anyhow.

5. According to the four schools, if one prays behind someone who is performing a full prayer, one must pray a full prayer.

6. According to the Hanbalis and Shafiʻis, if a traveller begins praying without having formulated the intention to abbreviate his prayer he must perform a complete prayer. According to

the Malikis, it is sufficient that a traveller formulate the intention of abbreviating his prayers the first time he prays during a journey. He does not have to renew his intention with every prayer. Hanafis say that a traveller's intention to abbreviate the prayer is not necessary. If one did not make the intention to abbreviate one must still do so, because the regulation regarding what is right and what is wrong does not alter with the intention, that is, that a traveller has already intended to make a journey.

7. For one to shorten one's prayers the Hanafis say that he must not intend to stay in a place for 15 consecutive days, or four days according to the Malikis and Shafi'is, or for a period containing more than 20 prayers according to the Hanbalis.

8. The Hanbalis say that if the occupation of the traveller requires that he travel constantly or requires him to be away from his home so that he is not at or near his home to perform his prayers he should not shorten his prayers.

9. Hanafis, Hanbalis and Malikis say that if a traveller is returning from his journey, intending to return to the place from which he began his travel, he must consider the distance that he is from it. If that distance is shorter than the prescribed distance, his condition of travel is nullified and he must pray in full. But if he had already covered the prescribed distance, he must abbreviate his prayers until he returns to his abode or city of residence.

The Shafi'i school holds that whenever one begins to return from his journey he must perform complete prayers even though he may be well beyond the prescribed distance.

# Bibliography

Agnon, S.Y., *The Days of Awe*. New York. Schocken Books, 1948.

Al-'Alawi, M., *Knowledge of God*. Translated by 'Abd al-Kabir al-Munawarra and 'Abd al-Sabur al-Ustadh., Norwich: Diwan Press, 1981.

'Ali, M., Trans. *The Holy Qur'an*. 6th ed. Chicago: Specialty Promotions, 1973.

Al-Amili, H., *Wasa'il al-Shi'ah*. Beirut. 1983.

Al-'Amuli, H., *Asrar al-Shari'ah wa Atwar al-Tariqah wa Anwar al-Haqiqah*. Tehran: Culture Studies and Research Institute, 1982.

Awliya'i, M., 'Outlines of the Development of the Science of Hadith.' *Al-Tawhid*, Vol.1, No.1.

Chakraborti, H., *Asceticism in Ancient India*. Calcutta: Punthi Pustak, 1973.

Cott, A., *Fasting: The Ultimate Diet*. New York: Bantam Books, 1979.

Cousens, G., *Spiritual Nutrition and the Rainbow Diet*. San Rafael: Cassandra Press, 1986.

Ad-Darqawi, A.Q., *The Hundred Steps*. Norwich: Diwan Press, 1979.

Edwards, G., *Hogmanay and Tiffany*. London: Geoffrey Bles Ltd., 1970.

'Fast of Ramadan', *Islamic Affairs*, Vol.7, Num.27 Feb. 1984: 1-3.

Gandhi, M.K., *Fasting in Satyagraha*. Ahmedabad: Narajivan Publishing House, 1965.

Goldstein, J., *Triumph Over Disease by Fasting and Natural Diet*. New York: Arco Publishing, 1977.

Gunning, P., *The Paschal or Lent Fast: Apostolical and Perpetual*. Oxford: John Henry Parker, 1845.

Haeri, F., *Beams of Illumination from the Divine Revelation*. London: Garnet Press, 1994.

Haeri, F., *Beginning's End*. London : KPI Ltd., 1987.

Haeri, F., *Al-Fiqh al-Mubassit*. London: Zahra Publications, 1986.

Hamaraneh, S., *Health Sciences in Early Islam*, Vols I and II. Ed. Munawar A. Anees. Blanco: Noor Health Foundation and Zahra Publications, 1983.

Hodgson, M., *The Venture of Islam*, Vol.I. Chicago: The University of Chicago Press, 1974.

*The Holy Bible*. London: Oxford University Press.

Al-Kashani, M.F., *Mahajjat al-Bayda' fi Tahdhib al-Ihya'*.

Kitov, E., *The Book of Our Heritage*. Jerusalem: 'A' Publishers, 1968.

Kushi, M., *The Book of Macrobiotics*. 10th ed. Tokyo: Japan Publications, 1977.

Mughniya, M.J., *Al-Fiqh al-Madhahib al-Khamsah*. Beirut: Dar al-Jawad, 1982.

Muramoto, N., *Healing Ourselves*. Ed. Michel Abehsera. New York: Avon Books, 1973.

Mutallib, M., *Riyad al-'Uqul*.

Al-Nasiri, M.B., *Mukhstasar Majmu' al-Bayan fi Tafsir al-Qur'an*. Beirut: Dar al-Zahra, 1980.

Qummi, A., *Mafatih al-Jinan*. Tehran.

Shakir, M.H., trans. *The Holy Qur'an*. New York: Tahrike Tarsile Qur'an, 1982.

Shelton, H.M., *Fasting Can Save Your Life*. 2nd ed. Chicago: Natural Hygiene Press, 1978.

Al-Tabataba'i, M.H. *Al-Mizan: An Exegesis of the Qur'an*. Trans. Sayyid Saeed Akhtar Rizvi. Vol 3. Tehran: WOFIS, 1982.

Al-Tabataba'i, M.H., *Al-Mizan fi Tafsir al-Qur'an*. Beirut, 1973.

Al-Zayyat, A. and al-Naysaburi, H., *Tibb al-A'immah*. Beirut: Dar al-Kitab al-Islami.